THE
EMERGENCE
OF
JEWISH
THEOLOGY
IN AMERICA

THE MODERN JEWISH EXPERIENCE

Paula Hyman and Deborah Dash Moore, *editors*

ROBERT G. GOLDY

THE
EMERGENCE
OF
JEWISH
THEOLOGY
IN AMERICA

INDIANA UNIVERSITY PRESS
Bloomington and Indianapolis

Manufactured in the United States of America

Library of Congress Cataloging-in-Publication Data

Goldy, Robert G.
The emergence of Jewish theology in America / Robert G. Goldy.
p. cm. — (The Modern Jewish experience
Bibliography: p.
Includes index.
ISBN 0-253-32601-X
1. Judaism—United States—Doctrines—History—20th century.
2. Judaism—20th century. I. Title. II Title: Jewish theology in
America. III. Series: Modern Jewish experience (Bloomington, Ind.)
BM205.G59   1990
296.3'0973—dc20   89-45417
CIP

1 2 3 4 5   94 93 92 91 90

CONTENTS

For my wife, Charlotte Ann,
and our daughter, Rachel Chana Ariel

Acknowledgments

The development of this work spans three time periods and geographical places. It began as a doctoral dissertation at the Hebrew University of Jerusalem. Most of the research for it took place in New York City at the Jewish Theological Seminary, Union Theological Seminary, and Columbia University. The manuscript was expanded and re-edited as a book at Miami University in Oxford, Ohio. I therefore want to gratefully acknowledge those persons and institutions who at each time and place contributed to the success of this endeavor.

I am indebted to the following institutions for helping to fund my research: the University of Haifa at Oranim, the Hebrew University of Jerusalem, the Jewish Theological Seminary, and the Memorial Foundation for Jewish Culture.

I want to thank for their teaching and good counsel Professors Nathan Rotenstreich, R. J. Zwi Werblowsky, Paul Mendes-Flohr, Eliezer Berkovits, David Hartman, and Eliezer Schweid. I also owe a great deal to the encouragement of my former *chaverim* in the kibbutz movement, especially Dit Dagan, Abraham Shapira, Ze'ev Levi, Yariv Ben Aharon, and Moshe Kerem.

My return after an absence of twelve years to the United States and my re-entry to the American Jewish community were made less difficult by the friendship and good will of a number of people: Professors Louis Finkelstein, Gerson Cohen, David Weiss-Halivni, Yochanan Muffs, Jules Harlow, Neil Gillman, Fritz Rothschild, Arthur Hyman, Eugene Borowitz; and those who have since passed away (may their memory be for a blessing), Professors Hershel Matt, Seymour Siegel, and Saul Lieberman. I am forever grateful to Lyndia Radice for her companionship and support. And my heartfelt gratitude goes to Mrs. Sylvia Heschel for her friendship and hospitality. Above all, I have a special love and appreciation for Professor Simon Greenberg and Mrs. Betty Greenberg to whom I owe more than I can express in words.

The transformation of the present work from a doctoral dissertation into a book has taken place with the encouragement of my friends and colleagues at Miami University, in the B'nai B'rith Hillel movement, and in the Rabbinate, especially Rabbis Steve Kaplan, Elliot Gertel, and Michael Brill. I am particularly appreciative for the professional help I have received from the editors and staff of the Indiana University Press, for the typing skills of Rhonda Rupel, the overall aid of Teresa Sweet, and the wit and wisdom of Dr. Ida Cohen Selavan, librarian at Hebrew Union College in Cincinnati. For their sound advice on ways to improve this work, I owe a special word of thanks to Professors Susannah Heschel, Arnold Eisen, David Ellenson, and my wife and intellectual companion, Professor Charlotte Newman Goldy. I dedicate this book to her and to our daughter.

THE
EMERGENCE
OF
JEWISH
THEOLOGY
IN AMERICA

1. INTRODUCTION

The study of Jewish theology has always been important for an understanding of Jewish history. It is a Diaspora phenomenon which has appeared in ancient Alexandria, medieval Spain, modern Germany, and after the Second World War in the United States. Irrespective of questions concerning the general value of theology for Judaism, or the worth of any particular theological work, the very fact that Jewish theology has developed on a significant scale in the United States makes it deserving of consideration within its historical context.

This book is best described as an intellectual history. In addition to examining the nature of the theological enterprise in America, it will treat the subject historically and comparatively, taking into account the social and historical forces which contributed to its development, as well as the intellectual factors, Jewish and Christian, European and American, that influenced its form and content.

Although such an approach is broad, the subject focuses on a single major issue: Jewish theology in the United States after the Second World War. It is further limited to one school of thought, the so-called new Jewish theology, and to four of its most important catalysts and representatives, Will Herberg, Abraham Joshua Heschel, Emil Fackenheim, and Joseph Soloveitchik.

More specifically, this study is devoted to the twofold task of examining the social, historical, and intellectual conditions for the emergence of Jewish theology in America, and discussing what four major American Jewish theologians understand to be the nature and function of Jewish theology. These points deserve elaboration.

The single most significant sociological condition for the development of Jewish theology in America was the emergence after the Second World War of a "third generation" of American Jews with a mind-set uniquely its own. Previous American generations had produced little original religious thought. What did exist of the latter was not theology in the strictest sense of the word. The "third generation" produced both theologians and an audience for theology.[1]

In this and similar studies, the expressions "second" and "third generation" are used in a special way, one that is accepted as standard usage in sociological literature on American Jewry.[2] These terms denote both a biological chain of familial succession from father to child to grandchild, and a unique outlook born of shared social experiences, concerns, and attitudes. Both of these uses of "generation" apply to American Jewry.

Although Jews have lived in America since 1654 and the institutional roots of the Jewish community date back at least to the middle of the nineteenth century, because of the massive immigration of Jews from Eastern Europe between 1880 and 1924 Jews coming of age in 1925–30 are considered "second generation," while those maturing about 1950–55 are called "third generation."[3]

More importantly, the expressions "second" and "third generation American" designate a particular outlook, consciousness, or mode of thought. According to contemporary social scientists, "the shared social experiences of age and peers are more critical in determining behavior than membership in the abstract category of generation of American nativity."[4] A particular theologian, therefore, can be regarded as a "third generation American" if he shared in that generation's ultimate questions and concerns and "joined in its debates and was subject to its influences," although he was not "biologically its native son in the strict sense of the term."[5]

Each generation, therefore, saw a particular work of Jewish religious thought as representative of its generation and typically "American." It did so, not solely because of the age or national origin of its author and the intellectual sources he employed, but primarily because the latter represented that generation and met its spiritual and intellectual needs. Mordecai Kaplan, for example, was not born in the United States. Nor was his thought based exclusively on American schools of sociology, philosophy, and Judaism. Yet he was considered by many within the "second generation" to be the most "American" of Jewish thinkers. Likewise, the theological views of Herberg, Heschel, Soloveitchik, and Fackenheim—as well as those of a younger generation of theologians such as Jakob Petuchowski, Fritz Rothschild, Steven Schwarzschild, and Michael Wyschogrod—were regarded by the postwar generation to be "third generation American," although these theologians were born in Europe, relied heavily on European schools of thought, and were not all of the same generation in age.

The Second World War (together with the events that led up to it) played an important historical role in the development of Jewish theology in America. The war's influence was twofold: it helped create among Jewish intellectuals a strong dissatisfaction with established forms of American Jewish thought, and it was responsible for the presence in North America of refugee scholars and theologians who represented new ways of thinking in religion.

The sociological condition of the "third generation" encouraged a tendency on the part of "third generation" American Jews to criticize modernity in general and modern Jewish thought in particular. Many postwar Jewish intellectuals exhibited a traditional, neo-Orthodox outlook, said to be typical of "third generation" Americans. Secure as modern Americans, they tended to be more critical of modernity and more appreciative of tradition than previous generations.[6] As Hansen and Herberg noted, in immigrant societies the children (the "third generation") wish to remember what the parents (the "second generation") wish to forget, namely, the traditional religious and ethnic heritage of the grandparents (the "first generation").[7]

The shared experience of the war further accentuated this tendency to criticize the modern world. Whether a soldier in the United States army (Irving Kristol), a student at a rabbinical seminary (Eugene Borowitz) or a refugee from Nazi Germany (Emil Fackenheim), many Jewish intellectuals came to believe that modern American Jewish thought was incompatible with the truths the war had taught them about God, man and the world.[8] They found it difficult to accept, for example, what they understood to be liberal Jewish notions concerning the absolute perfectibility of human nature and the inevitable progress of human history toward the Rational and the Good. American Judaism, they argued, did not deal adequately with the problem of evil; nor had it room for belief in the living and redeeming, supernatural God of Jewish tradition. For many postwar Jewish intellectuals, the modern era in history—with all its forms of religious and secular thinking—came to an end with the Second World War. Jews were in crisis in the modern world. This was the case physically for the survivors of Nazism who had to be resettled in Europe, America, and Palestine. The postwar generation believed it was even more the case spiritually: modernity itself was in crisis, and with it the whole of modern Jewish thought.

At a time when young Jews were seeking alternatives to established ways of thinking, the war and the events that preceded it accounted for the presence in North America of a significant number of important refugee scholars and theologians, many of whom represented major schools of European philosophy and theology.[9] The younger generation came into contact with these refugees on university campuses and at rabbinical seminaries, through their writings and public addresses. To these young people, they appeared as heroic figures: exiled prophets, armed with teachings that might redeem humanity.

At the same time, it must be noted that the two historical events Jews most often associated with the war—the Holocaust and the reborn Jewish state—were not important theological issues until after the 1967 Arab-Israeli War.[10] Before that time, religious thinkers spoke of the "tragedies," "horrors," and "lessons" of the war in general terms. Even when these issues did become part of the theological agenda in America, only a few major theologians (Emil Fackenheim, Richard Rubenstein, and Eliezer Berkovits) fully devoted themselves to an analysis of the meaning of the Holocaust and the reestablished Jewish state for the future of Jewish theological thinking.

After the Second World War, the writing of Jewish theology was fostered by the Protestant theological revival that began in America during the early 1930s and reached its peak by the end of the war, the growing availability of translations of and commentaries on the writings of European Jewish theologians, and the establishment of prominent Jewish journals that served as important media for theological discussion and debate.

Between 1945 and 1950, prospective Jewish theologians had no real precedent to follow. American Jewry had produced little original theology. Heschel, Fackenheim, and Soloveitchik had not yet published major works in English. Herberg and Steinberg had published some exploratory essays on the subject of Jewish and Protestant theology, but were still engaged primarily in the study of current trends in theology.[11] The only theological sources readily available in English were Christian, namely, the writings of Reinhold Niebuhr and translations of works by Karl Barth, Emil Brunner, Nicolai Berdyaev, Paul Tillich, Soren Kierkegaard, and Rudolf Bultmann.

Niebuhr was responsible for reviving Protestant theology in America and replacing existing schools of liberal and naturalistic thinking with his own brand of neo-Orthodoxy. His popularity and influence were immense, reaching into all areas of American intellectual life.[12] It was due to Niebuhr's personal influence that Herberg found his way back to Judaism and became an important Jewish theologian.[13] And, with Niebuhr as their mentor, the younger generation of Jewish theologians was able to acquire valuable lessons in theology and theological writing, as well as a lasting appreciation for the contributions of other Christian thinkers—Tillich, Barth, and Kierkegaard, in particular.[14]

Models of European Jewish theology existed, but were not easily accessible to American Jews. Initiated by Franz Rosenzweig and Martin Buber, a revival of Jewish theology took place in Europe immediately after the First World War. Most American Jews did not become aware of these new theological trends for quite some time. Notoriously weak in the knowledge of foreign languages, Americans in general and American Jews in particular came to know of the contributions of Rosenzweig and Buber only when translations of their writings began to appear, slowly during the 1940s and with increased momentum thereafter.[15] By 1955 the writings of Buber, and to a lesser degree, Rosenzweig, had become well known in the United States. Nahum Glatzer, Maurice Friedman, and Will Herberg published important collections and studies of their work.[16] And Buber's three visits to the United States during the 1950s gave further impetus to his and Rosenzweig's growing popularity.[17]

A 1945 survey of rabbinic opinion in America showed Mordecai Kaplan's type of religious naturalism to be the single greatest influence on American Jewish thought. By 1965–66, there were indications that Kaplan's influence had been superseded by that of Buber and Rosenzweig.[18]

Another important factor in the development of Jewish theological activity in America was the creation after the war of important Jewish journals, which served as an open forum for theological expression and debate. The most important of these were *Commentary* and *Judaism.* Nonsectarian in nature, they were able to reach a wider audience than most existing Jewish publications which dealt primarily with narrowly defined denominational issues, more ideological than theological in nature.[19]

The decade of the 1950s marked a period of intellectual ferment within the Jewish intellectual community. In the pages of *Commentary, Judaism,* and other Jewish journals, as well as in classrooms and at rabbinical conferences, Herberg, Heschel, Fackenheim, and a group of young theologians openly challenged the hegemony of religious liberalism within the Reform and Conservative movements.[20] When the rabbinic leadership responded, there took place in Jewish journals a number of controversial debates, focused on the views of specific personalities, particularly Buber and Rosenzweig, Herberg and Heschel, Niebuhr and Steinberg.[21] This period of controversy came to an end between 1960 and 1965, at which time it was generally acknowledged that "the new Jewish theology" had become a dominant intellectual force within American Judaism.

The initiators of this intellectual revolution in American Jewish thought—Will Herberg, A. J. Heschel, Emil Fackenheim, and Joseph Soloveitchik—became known as the fathers of the new Jewish theology, and the mentors of a new generation of Conservative, Reform, and Orthodox theologians. They were among the first to champion the cause of Jewish theology in America. Given the strong antitheological bias that prevailed in the established Jewish community, they sought to win legitimacy for their discipline, to create original theologies of their own, and to outline the basic principles for writing Jewish theology that others could follow.

It is with this in mind that the present study attempts to do more than locate the social, historical, and intellectual factors that made it possible for

Jewish theology to develop in the United States, and to describe how its proponents emerged victorious in their debates with the champions of established Jewish thinking. *How* Jewish theology came about and *why* it took the direction it did are important considerations. Equally so, however, is an examination of *what* major Jewish theologians regarded as the nature and function of their theological enterprise, and what it was that made them believe their writings were authentically Jewish and vitally significant for contemporary American Jewry.

The first aim of this study, namely, a description of the conditions under which Jewish theology developed in America after 1945, and the resulting struggle which took place within the intellectual community, will be discussed in chapters two through five. Its second aim, the analysis of the views of Herberg and Heschel, Fackenheim and Soloveitchik on the writing of Jewish theology, will be dealt with in chapters six and seven. Chapter eight will briefly survey the course Jewish theology has taken since its beginnings after the Second World War.

2. THE SITUATION OF AMERICAN JEWISH THEOLOGY IN 1945

Historically, Jewish theology has arisen at times when the Jewish people lived in, and were able to freely interact with, a highly developed non-Jewish culture. This at least was the case in ancient Alexandria, medieval Spain, and modern Germany.[1] It would seem to follow, then, that it would be the case in the United States. For a time, however, the contrary seemed to be true. Before 1945, American-Jewish life was, as characterized by Arthur Cohen, known for "its consistent, stubborn, and—given the intellectual revolutions of the twentieth century—almost miraculous avoidance of theology."[2] According to Ira Eisenstein, American Jewry "had generated organizations and institutions, and had developed individuals whose major concerns had been philanthropy, the upbuilding of Zion, resisting anti-Semitism, and perfecting the art of 'community relations.'" It did not produce "thoughtful and scholarly writers" who would devote their attention to "the fundamentals of human existence."[3] Lou Silberman and Arnold Eisen have written that because "American Jews attempted no serious assessment of the intellectual structure of Jewish existence,"[4] a situation resulted in which "American Jewish theology was virtually non-existent."[5]

In addition to the paucity of theological literature, there was little theology being taught at the rabbinical schools before 1945. A situation existed in which there were Jewish theological seminaries with no theology.[6] At the seminaries, Borowitz, Cohon, and Himmelfarb have maintained, there was a widespread "antipathy"[7] and "antagonism"[8]—a "sneering at the theological enterprise."[9] When, in 1923, Samuel Cohon inherited Kaufmann Kohler's chair of Jewish theology at Hebrew Union College, the atmosphere at the college was charged with hostility toward Jewish theology. Cohon wrote:

> Proposals were urged to alter its name to something more euphonious and less committed to theistic presuppositions. It therefore became necessary to demonstrate the religious nature of Judaism and the role of

theology in its development, as well as to justify the place of theology in
the curriculum of a rabbinical seminary.[10]

In spite of this attitude, Hebrew Union College did more than other
major seminaries to provide students with a knowledge of Jewish philosophy and theology. For example, the college's first two presidents, Isaac
Mayer Wise and Kaufmann Kohler, saw themselves as theologians, and a
department of Jewish theology was established early in the institution's
history. In addition, the college employed on its teaching staff such noted
religious thinkers as David Neumark, Samuel Atlas, Samuel Cohon, Leo
Baeck, and A. J. Heschel. Yet after his visit to Hebrew Union College in
1947, Will Herberg wrote: "They take theology seriously at H.U.C., but
unfortunately their theology is not very serious."[11]

Herberg's impression was shared by many of the rabbi-theologians who
studied at the college in the 1940s.[12] It was not so much the lack of theology
that they objected to, but the type that was taught. In their opinion, it was
arrested in outdated modes of thinking, primarily nineteenth-century German idealism, and did not take into account the new trends in European
thought.[13] As such, it did not actively respond to the issues of the day: the
horrors of the war, anti-Semitism, the depths of human evil and depravity,
the problems of self-transcendence and Jewish identity. Although Heschel
and Baeck taught for a short time at Hebrew Union College neither dealt
with contemporary theology. Heschel taught medieval thought, Baeck,
Midrash.

A like situation existed at the Conservative movement's Jewish Theological Seminary. Professor Louis Ginzberg was deeply concerned about
the lack of Jewish philosophy and theology in the Seminary's rabbinic curriculum. Prior to and during the First World War, he did his best to amend
this situation. In a letter to the institution's president, Solomon Schechter,
he deplored the state of the students' ignorance of theology and suggested
something be done about it. On another occasion, Ginzberg addressed a
long memorandum to the seminary's president and faculty, recommending
a sizeable expansion of this phase of the curriculum. However, little seems
to have resulted from his efforts.[14] Until 1945, there was neither a department of Jewish theology, nor regularly given courses in Jewish theology
at the seminary. In the absence of such courses a student could, however,
submit an independently written paper on the subject of Jewish philosophy
or theology to a professor, especially Mordecai Kaplan or Louis Ginzberg.[15]
Schechter and Louis Finkelstein, who were trained as historians rather than
theologians, occasionally dealt with theological issues in their classes. But

in Finkelstein's opinion neither he nor Schechter taught courses which could be strictly defined as theology.[16]

The situation was quite similar at Yeshiva University's Rabbi Isaac El-chanan Theological Seminary. Although Isaac Husik taught medieval Jew-ish philosophy for a short period in the 1920s and Joseph Soloveitchik touched upon theological issues in some of his classes in Talmud, there was no department of philosophy or theology at Yeshiva University prior to the Second World War. Nor were courses in these fields a regular part of the rabbinic curriculum.[17]

According to most observers of the religious situation in America, the achievement of Jewish theology prior to 1945 was not commensurate with its potential. Simon Noveck wrote:

> Until the Second World War, Jewish thought in the United States had neither the passion and fire of that of Russian Jewry, nor the profundity and depth of German Jewry's intellectual spokesmen. Aside from Solo-mon Schechter, Mordecai M. Kaplan and Kaufmann Kohler, there were few original theological thinkers in American Jewry. Nor were there any attempts to develop comprehensive systems of thought in the manner of Ahad Ha-am, Simon Dubnow, or Martin Buber to serve as a guide to the perplexed of our generation.[18]

While there is general agreement about the condition of Jewish theology in America preceding the Second World War, explanations of the reasons for that condition diverge. The reasons most often given, however, can be grouped within four general arguments, namely, the argument from prag-matism, the argument from communal welfare, the argument from mo-dernity, and the argument from tradition.

I.

The argument from pragmatism takes several forms, all of which share the view that the sorry state of Jewish theology can be attributed to practical considerations which give higher priority to doing than to thinking. It is often argued, for instance, that American Jews have been affected by the general anti-intellectual, "pragmatic" outlook of the American people.[19] Born of the immigrant-pioneering experience, this attitude allegedly shuns theoretical endeavors by encouraging activity rather than introspection. Wrote Noveck, "This pragmatism is reflected in the American synagogue and in the sermons of American rabbis, who until recently, carefully avoided theological themes."[20] Silberman pointed out that it is found, too, in "an anti-intellectual stance that has regarded theology as at best a luxury, at worst, sheer drivel."[21]

The pragmatic outlook, this argument maintains, was further reinforced by the situation of the first and second generation of American Jews who, before 1945, were absorbed with the practical demands of integration into American society. As such, immediate social and economic needs took precedence over theoretical concerns.[22] The American rabbinate responded to this situation by stressing the practical aspects of the profession—social work, counseling, fund-raising—rather than scholarship and theory for its own sake. Eugene Borowitz wrote that because they believed that theology has little to do with practical questions, "the leadership of what is purportedly the Jewish religious community is, as a whole, uninterested in theology."[23]

By the time American Jewry had begun to achieve a measure of social integration and economic security, it was compelled by historical events to devote its psychic energies even more to practical affairs. Wrote Silberman:

> Confronted by the enormity of the Jewish disaster of the 1930s and 1940s; involved in rescue and rehabilitation of the remnant; concerned with political problems and the Palestinian community; filled with enthusiasm at the emergence of the State of Israel and its survival; American Jews attempted no serious assessment of the intellectual structures of Jewish existence.[24]

Given the above circumstances, it seemed only natural that American Jews would be more interested in hearing about the problems of the Jewish people than in speculation concerning the question of God. To them, as Arthur Cohen has written, "theology appeared either frivolous or tragically wasteful."[25]

There are still other practical reasons given for the failure of American Jewry to devote itself more fully to the theological enterprise. In addition to the insufficient recognition of the significance of theology and of its role in Jewish life, there was a serious scarcity of Jewish scholars in general and of Jewish theologians in particular. This situation has been attributed to two factors. First, there were few academic positions available either inside or outside of the Jewish community which would allow for thinkers to devote themselves wholly to the problems of Jewish culture and thought. Consequently, as Samuel Cohon complained at the time, "our most gifted minds direct their attention to other fields."[26] Second, it was the opinion of some that the overly practical orientation of the rabbinical seminaries helped produce a generation of rabbis who were unqualified to understand and write about theological issues. Arnold Eisen has pointed out that "rabbis and their few lay counterparts in Jewish theological circles during the period were 'middle-brow', at best. They simply did not have the tools to do theology, and even those equipped to do theology were unequipped to do *Jewish* theology."[27] In a 1947 letter to the editors of *Commentary*, Robert Gordis asked why American Jewry had not produced a significant philosophical literature and noted that:

> The lack of such a literature today is not accidental. In the first instance, the past hundred and fifty years since the French Revolution have de-Judaized most of the creative Jewish spirits in Western Europe and America, so that with few exceptions, the thinkers among them do not know Judaism, while those who know Judaism are rarely creative thinkers.[28]

According to David Novack, Heschel "used to bemoan the fact that most of the *talmidei hakhamim* were disinterested in philosophy and ignorant of it, and most of the so-called Jewish philosophers were *amei ha'aretz*."[29]

Ideally, to engage in Jewish theology a rabbi would be required to have advanced training in philosophical methodologies, a grounding in traditional sources (halakha as well as aggada), and an acquaintance with the history of Jewish and non-Jewish theology. During the period under consideration, however, most rabbinical seminaries in America provided little of the first, increasingly less of the second, and close to nothing of the third.[30]

It must be noted, as well, that few American-educated rabbis possessed the language skills necessary to gain a firm grounding in theological literature. Modern Jewish religious thought is very much the product of German language and culture. In Milton Himmelfarb's words, "All modern Jews—insofar as they are modern, or even post-modern—walk in the footsteps of German-speaking Jewry, the pioneers of Jewish modernity."[31] Yet few American rabbis knew German well enough to read and understand a philosophical text in that language.

This linguistic narrowness should not be underestimated. The translation of German-Jewish literature did not take place on a wide scale until after 1945. Until then, the major part of nineteenth- and twentieth-century Jewish and non-Jewish philosophy and religious thought was inaccessible to most American thinkers. Many rabbis, therefore, could only pay "formal obeisance" to the thought of Mendelssohn, Geiger, Cohen, Rosenzweig, and Buber.[32]

II.

The argument from communal welfare has been expressed in a variety of ways, all of which treat theology as a potential threat to the welfare of the Jewish community in the United States.

One version of this argument underscores the potential danger a well-defined Jewish theology would pose for Jewish-Christian relations. Judd Teller conceived of theology as a fundamentally otherworldly enterprise, and suggested that by opposing those secular values that have made it possible for American Jews to live a more secure and decent life than Jews have known in any other place in the Diaspora, Jewish theology would jeopardize "the great gains of the Jew in American society," and even encourage the forces of anti-Semitism.[33]

Another version of the argument from communal welfare focuses upon the possible danger a Jewish theology (conceived of exclusively in terms of the dogmatic model of medieval scholasticism) might present to the internal stability of the Jewish religious community, divided as it is along denominational lines. In the Conservative movement, for example, it was argued that a clearly defined and authoritative "Conservative philosophy" would weaken the movement's commitment to the principles of religious pluralism and create a kind of inner polarization and factionalism that would jeopardize its claim to being a viable alternative to Reform and Orthodox Judaism.[34]

III.

A third argument often used to explain why Jewish theology did not play an important role in American Jewish life prior to the Second World War is the argument from modernity.

The emergence of the modern era has often been interpreted as a victory of modernism over medievalism, a victory of the ideals of human freedom, reason, and autonomy over those of religious authoritarianism, divine revelation, and heteronomy. Modernity, therefore, marked a reversal of priorities, replacing supernaturalism with naturalism (or, phenomenalism), theoretical or metaphysical reason with practical, functional reason, and, as a result, theology and metaphysics with science and technology.[35]

Products of the modern era, the major denominations in American Judaism proudly maintained that they had discovered ways in which to reconcile tradition with modernity.[36] This was especially important for those first and second generation Jews for whom "becoming modern" appeared to be synonymous with acceptance and success—with becoming truly "American."

The argument from modernity contends that Jewish theology did not gain a foothold prior to 1945 because, for most modern Jews and Christians, theology was associated with a premodern world of church dogmatism and religious supernaturalism. This is why the word "theology" was unpopular.[37] According to Jacob Petuchowski, it sounded too "narrow and medieval, when contrasted with such more respectable and acceptable terms as 'religious philosophy' and 'religious thought.' "[38] Borowitz wrote that at Hebrew Union College, "everyone was for religion and against theology,"[39] and, as Cohon maintained, "proposals were urged to alter its name to something more euphonius and less committed to theistic presuppositions."[40]

IV.

The argument from tradition is perhaps the most commonly given explanation for the neglect of Jewish theology. According to it, the situation of American Jewish theology was simply an expression of the fact that traditionally, Judaism has never put great emphasis on theology as such. Theology, it is maintained, is not indigenous to Judaism; it is alien to the overall Jewish spirit.[41] This is purportedly so for several reasons. First, Noveck wrote, "rabbinic authorities have been wary about theological speculation, regarding *Halakhah,* and the practice of the Jewish way of life as more important."[42] According to Borowitz, American rabbis have opposed theology because it "smacked of 'pie in the sky' and was viewed with the traditional skepticism towards preoccupation with hidden things when there was so much to be done with what had already been revealed."[43]

Second, since theology, it was held, is rigid and dogmatic, and Judaism is allegedly an undogmatic religion, theology was said to be alien to the Jewish spirit. As Borowitz has maintained, the rabbis feared that if a Jewish theology arose the "next step would be to seek conformity to it, to force it upon others and thus destroy that productive pluralism, that creative intellectual dialectic which has been so precious a Jewish heritage."[44]

Third, the argument from tradition maintains that, as Moshe Davis has argued, "the Jews (with notable exceptions) did not, historically, concentrate on systematic theological thought in their literature" because "traditionally,

Jewish ideas had been derived from the study of the classical texts and were expressed through commentaries on these texts."[45] It is held, therefore, that although contemporary Jewish theology did not exist, for the most part, as an independent, systematically conceived discipline, it was to be found within traditional rabbinic literature—in prayers and sermons, aggadic tales, and midrashic interpretations of the Bible.[46]

The minimal attention devoted to Jewish theology at rabbinical seminaries prior to the Second World War is sometimes justified on the grounds that quantitatively and qualitatively, theology is not on a par with traditional Jewish subjects. According to Finkelstein and Kaplan, theology forms a very small part of the Jewish intellectual heritage and did not, therefore, warrant the attention usually reserved for the study of rabbinic subjects.[47] Moreover, Saul Lieberman has maintained, Jewish theology tends to be popular and apologetic, lacking in the rigor and sophistication found in the areas of Jewish history and linguistics, Bible and Talmud.[48]

Only when taken together do the above four arguments provide an explanation for this neglect of Jewish theology. Individually, each is limited and inadequate. Moreover, their significance often lies more in what they do not, rather than in what they do say.

While it is true, for example, that American Jewry was deeply concerned with the pressing practical issues of the time, this does not in itself explain why Jewish theology should have been neglected. Often in Jewish history, the concern for survival in times of crisis has actually served to encourage theological activity.[49] Furthermore, the pragmatic argument does not account for the fact that while Jewish theology was being neglected and even disparaged, *theoretical* work in the areas of Talmud, Midrash, and Jewish history was not.[50]

The pragmatic argument presupposes a limited notion of theory in general, and theology in particular. Because it implies that theory has little effect on practice, theology—understood as a purely speculative and otherworldly activity—is judged to have limited social value, especially in times of crisis.

In contrast, the argument from communal welfare attributes great social effectiveness to theology; it conceives of the latter, however, in wholly negative terms. Understood as a dogmatic and authoritarian enterprise designed to achieve uniformity in thought and behavior, theology is judged to be incompatible with the democratic, undogmatic principles of Jewish tradition and modern American society. Conceived of primarily in denominational and ideological ways, theology is condemned, too, as a potential cause of conflict both within a particular Jewish denomination (viz., the Conservative movement) and between Jewish and Christian denominations in

America. The possibility and value of theological pluralism is hardly considered, nor is the conception of theology as a discipline devoted to the pursuit of religious truth.

In addition to harboring restricted views of theology, the arguments from pragmatism and communal welfare often contain a hidden value judgment. By employing what philosophers call an inference from an *is* to an *ought* (and which many take to be an illegitimate inference), it is implied that because theology *has not been* an integral part of Jewish intellectual life in America, it therefore *ought not* to be. The paucity of Jewish theology is thereby transformed, as Abraham Karp put it, from an "embarrassment into a virtue."[51]

The above two arguments claim to account for the situation of Jewish theology by stressing its incompatibility with the practical concerns of the Jewish community. Upon closer examination, however, it appears that while practical considerations were involved, the lack of theology was caused more than anything else by an antitheological bias engendered by specific conceptions of the nature and function of theology.

In the arguments from tradition and modernity, it is not only narrowly conceived notions of "theology" that proved to be obstacles to the development of an American Jewish theology, but specific conceptions, as well, of the meaning of "modernity" and "tradition."

Although antithetical in some respects, contemporary ideas of modernity and tradition share a common tendency toward religious reductionism which serves to eliminate Jewish theology as an independent discipline. Thus, both approaches reduce theological issues to practical ethical concerns, and interpret them by means of *modern* science (psychology, sociology, natural science, linguistics) or moral philosophy (usually Kantian or Deweyan) and/or *traditional* sources (halakhic and aggadic). In this way, theology is replaced by modern and traditional disciplines; and theological issues are located and dealt with, not so much in theological texts such as the writings of Philo, Maimonides, Saadia, Mendelssohn, Cohen, Buber, or Rosenzweig, but rather, where (it is implied) they belong, namely, in traditional literature: the Bible, Talmud, and Midrash, in sermons, eulogies, poetry, and prayers.

The above discussion outlines attitudes toward Jewish theology in America before 1945. The situation began to change after the Second World War, when a growing number of voices called for the revival of Jewish theology. Concerned primarily with the question of God (especially with ways to rediscover the biblical faith in a living and saving, personal God) the champions of Jewish theology first turned their attention to the subject of theology itself, hoping thereby to acquire the means by which to

talk about the Divine. In so doing, they were challenged to demonstrate
the independence and authenticity of Jewish theology and to prove its
legitimacy and relevance for a community preoccupied with "survivalist"
issues. They also had to surmount both modern and traditional objections
to theology and to discover a theological "third way" which went beyond
existing forms of liberalism and orthodoxy. In working toward this end,
they quite naturally looked for precedents to guide them in the writings
of Martin Buber and Franz Rosenzweig, Paul Tillich and Karl Barth. The
new generation of American Jewish theologians felt a strong kinship with
the thought and personalities of these thinkers. In both cases the break
with religious liberalism came about as the direct result of a world war, the
First World War in Europe, the Second World War in the United States.
Furthermore, these European theologians appeared to share with young
Americans a "third generation" disposition. If the generation of Mendelssohn and Schleiermacher is the first generation of modern European theologians, and that of Hermann Cohen and Adolf Harnack the second, then
Buber, Rosenzweig, Tillich, and Barth were "third generation" thinkers.
They certainly exhibited an important characteristic of the latter, namely,
a theological outlook that is postmodern, neo-orthodox, and existentialist.[52]

What began as a simple appeal for increased theological activity soon
developed into a major confrontation between a new kind of theology and
the prevailing religious liberalism that had dominated American Jewish
thought for generations. The confrontation would last for over a decade,
forming one of the most interesting periods in American Jewish intellectual
history.

3. THE CALL FOR THEOLOGY

Like many important contributors to Jewish religious thinking in the twentieth century, Will Herberg had first to traverse the way of secular modernism before he could turn to a life devoted to Jewish thought and practice. Herberg was not a rabbi, nor was he raised in a religious home. In regard to Judaism, he began as an "outsider" and became a celebrated *ba'al teshuva*.

Herberg was born into a Russian-Jewish family which came to America at the turn of the twentieth century. His parents, whom he described as passionate atheists and ardent socialists, carefully educated their son to believe as they did. As a young man, he joined the American Communist party and became the editor of its chief ideological publications.[1] By 1929 he had broken with the party, and in 1937 with Marxist philosophy. It was at this time that he discovered the writings of Reinhold Niebuhr. Herberg wrote:

> My first encounter with the thought of Reinhold Niebuhr came in the late 1930s. I was then at a most crucial moment in my life. My Marxist faith had collapsed under the shattering blows of contemporary history. . . . I was left literally without any ground to stand on, deprived of the commitment and understanding that alone had made life liveable. At this point, in a way I cannot now remember, I came upon Niebuhr's *Moral Man and Immoral Society*. . . . It came with the revelation of a new understanding of human existence in terms of which I might reconstruct my life and thought. . . . Humanly speaking, it 'converted' me, for in some manner I cannot describe, I felt my whole being, and not merely my thinking, shifted to a new center. I could now speak about God and religion without embarrassment.[2]

Niebuhr was the leading proponent of neo-orthodox theology in America. His book *Moral Man and Immoral Society* had an explosive effect on theology in America, paralleling that which Barth's commentary on the Epistle to the Romans had in Europe after the First World War. According to Bob Patterson, "no other book in the first third of the twentieth century had a greater impact in American theological circles."[3] Nor, for that matter, did a book in theology have such a powerful influence on secular intellectuals. Well-known political, economic, social, and historical thinkers also claimed Niebuhr as their mentor, Norman Thomas, George Kennan, Walter Reuther, Walter Lippmann, Arthur Schlesinger, Jr., Robert Oppenheimer, Lionell Trilling, James Reston, and Kenneth Galbraith among them. Naturalists such as John Dewey, Sidney Hook, Horace Kallen, and Henry Nelson Weiman defended secular and religious naturalism against Niebuhr's neo-orthodox supernaturalism.[4]

It was by means of Niebuhr's writings that Herberg found his way to religion, and by the force of Niebuhr's personal guidance that he discovered his vocation as a Jewish theologian. When at their first meeting, Herberg declared his intention of becoming a Christian, Niebuhr encouraged him to remain a Jew, recommending that he go to the Jewish Theological Seminary. Although he never enrolled as a student, Herberg's association with the seminary provided him with the grounding he lacked. On an informal basis, some professors and students undertook to instruct Herberg in Hebrew and Jewish thought.[5] Seymour Siegel wrote that, "very soon the brilliant pupil, filled with enthusiasm of discovery, became the teacher. He began to write on Jewish theology for periodicals such as *Jewish Frontier* and *Commentary*. He had found his mission in life and pursued it with the zeal of a biblical prophet."[6] Invited by Louis Finkelstein in 1946 to participate in a series of seminary symposia entitled "My Faith as a Jew," Herberg delivered a paper that was published a year later in *Commentary* as "From Marxism to Judaism."[7] This essay launched him on his theological career and brought his work to the attention of Milton Steinberg, with whom Herberg was to form a relationship that would help change the course of Jewish thought in America.[8]

II.

Milton Steinberg was one of the most eloquent and persuasive popularizers of liberal Judaism in America. Although a Reconstructionist, he was critical of what he considered to be the weaknesses in Kaplan's thought, especially his failure to formulate an adequate philosophical rationale.[9] Silberman wrote that because Steinberg was trained in classical languages and philosophy, he "took the classical philosophical enterprise seriously at a time when many of his contemporaries had hearkened to the siren call of sociology and had erected the structure of their religious thought on the more popular platform of non- or anti-philosophy."[10] Steinberg was convinced that man's "metaphysical hunger" could not be denied and theology could not be replaced by sociology.[11]

In spite of his growing uneasiness with liberal Judaism, Steinberg's published views were almost indistinguishable from the status quo in American liberal thought. Thus, when his *Basic Judaism* appeared in 1947, a young *Commentary* editor, Irving Kristol, wrote a scathing attack on it and the kind of Judaism it represented. Recently discharged from the American army and eager to re-evaluate his war experience in light of the Jewish heritage, Kristol asked: "What does contemporary Jewish theology have to offer people like me?"—namely, those young people who after the war, had come to feel a desperate sense of crisis and castastrophe, of "walking off the cliff-edge that is the 20th-century."[12] Expressing his disappointment, Kristol strongly condemned Steinberg's liberalism, "the state of mind of a large section of the American rabbinate and much of the American Jewish community in general," as a "perversion of the Jewish religion into a shallow, if sincere, humanitarianism, plus a thorough-going insensitivity to present-day spiritual problems."[13]

Steinberg was one of the only liberal Jewish thinkers of his generation to accept Kristol's challenge. A man for whom the philosopher's search for truth was of paramount importance, he began to earnestly re-examine the fundamentals of his religious liberalism in light of the current trends in Continental and American philosophy and theology.[14] Although this project was cut short by Steinberg's untimely death in 1950, it represented what Silberman considered "one of the few vigorous confrontations of contemporary theological thought by a Jewish scholar that took place in the decade of the '40s."[15]

By 1949, articles by Herberg, Fackenheim, Heschel, and Buber were appearing regularly in important journals. A revival of Protestant theology in America had been sparked by the growing influence of the writings of Kierkegaard, Barth, Tillich, Brunner, Maritain and the Niebuhr brothers. With this in mind, the members of the Rabbinical Assembly of America—the organization of those rabbis affiliated with the Conservative movement—invited Steinberg to deliver a paper to their annual convention which would survey trends in Protestant and Jewish theology. Noveck wrote:

> It was a complex, scholarly assignment, involving a program of reading few rabbis at the time were qualified to undertake. Today . . . Buber and Rosenzweig are well known in the Jewish community, and the works of Barth, Brunner, Heidegger, the two Niebuhrs and Tillich are available in paperbacks. In 1949 most rabbis were just becoming aware of these

names. It was no mean feat for Steinberg to synthesize the various theological currents into a coherent paper and present his own evaluation.[16]

At Steinberg's suggestion, Will Herberg was included in the program as
a respondent. In his remarks, Herberg reminded his audience that secular
cults such as communism and fascism, scientism and psychologism, were
"making their bid—with devastating success—for the soul of the bewildered
and disoriented man of our time." Only a vitally new theology, "a living
theology . . . built upon Scripture and the materials of Jewish religious tradition," could satisfy the "growing hunger for something that will render
life significant in ultimate terms, for something beyond the shallow for-
mulas and the once plausible half-truths of naturalism."[17]

Herberg concluded his remarks by stressing the need for a God-centered
theology which would help convey the word of God to the modern world.
He declared:

> We need this theology and we need it most urgently. The rabbi is ap-
> pointed to preach the word of God and to guide his community in ac-
> cordance with it. We all, rabbi and layman alike, must live by it. To search
> for the word of God, to try to understand and interpret it for our time:
> that is our theological task. May this discussion here today mark the be-
> ginning of a new creative effort on the part of American Jewry to meet
> and fulfill it.[18]

Steinberg was too ill to attend the convention; his paper was read by his
good friend, Judah Goldin. Referring to Herberg's call for the revival of
Jewish theology, Steinberg maintained that

> A need exists, a great and crying need, for just that analytical exposition
> of the Jewish religious outlook to which this exhortation summons us.
> Failing it, Judaism will be poorer and less nourishing than it should and
> can be. It will, therefore, be less capable of eliciting the loyalty and dedi-
> cation of better Jewish minds and hearts, which in consequence will depart
> from it into a religious wasteland, if indeed they do not make their way
> into those Christian communions which do furnish the required spiritual
> nutriment. In this sense, Mr. Herberg's challenge concerns itself with a
> factor in Jewish survival as consequential in the long run as those "prac-
> tical" issues on which American Jewry as a whole, its rabbis included, are
> wont to expend themselves.[19]

The response to Steinberg and Herberg's call for increased theological
activity was far from enthusiastic. Eugene Kohn, a leading representative
of the Reconstructionist point of view, presented a paper in which he defended the naturalist orientation of the majority of rabbis at the conven-

tion.[20] Reflecting Kaplan's outlook, he argued that sociology, not philosophy and theology, would best serve the spiritual needs of the American Jewish community. As for the reaction of the audience, friends of Herberg and Steinberg have contended that the rabbis were either uninterested in the theological nature of the topic, or bored by such a lengthy presentation. There were some, it is held, that treated the call for theology as scandalous, especially when asked to consider sympathetically the models of Christian and existentialist thought.[21]

III.

Invited to participate in a symposium on the subject of prayer at the 1953 convention of the Rabbinical Assembly, Abraham Joshua Heschel took the opportunity to add his voice to those, who like Herberg and Steinberg, were calling for a re-examination of liberal Judaism.[22] Although a professor at the Jewish Theological Seminary since 1945, Heschel addressed his audience as a relative outsider.[23] Scion of a Hasidic dynasty in Poland and possessor of a doctorate in philosophy from the University of Berlin, Heschel espoused a brand of Judaism that ran counter to the mainstream of American Judaism. His outlook was biblical rather than modern, supernaturalist and mystic rather than naturalist and rationalist. His thought was theological, expressed in terms of the Continental philosophies of phenomenology and existentialism. The prevailing school of American Jewish thought was antitheological, formulated in the categories of psychology, sociology, and pragmatist philosophy.

Whereas Herberg and Steinberg became acquainted with the new thinking in Continental theology and philosophy toward the end of the Second World War, Heschel witnessed its development where and when it began in Germany between the world wars. Together with Emil Fackenheim and Joseph Soloveitchik, he was part of a younger generation of Jewish theologians who were heirs to the revival in Jewish and Protestant thought that had taken place in Europe.

In *Man is Not Alone*, Heschel insisted that modern man no longer knows how to ask the right questions. When asked, therefore, to speak at the Rabbinical Assembly convention about synagogue worship, Heschel chose to speak about theology and the question of God.[24] He opened his address to the assembled rabbis by asking:

> Now what qualifies a person to be a rabbi? What gives him the right, the privilege to represent the Word of God to the people of God? I have been

in the United States of America for thirteen years. I have not discovered
America, but I have discovered something in America. It is possible to be
a rabbi and not to believe in the God of Abraham, Isaac and Jacob.[25]

Heschel is referring here to Joseph Zeitlin's 1945 study which purported
to show that the majority of Reform and Conservative rabbis were naturalists who replaced the biblical notion of a personal, supernatural God
with a variety of modern conceptions.[26] For Heschel, naturalist religion is
a form of "religious solipsism" which stifles prayer by turning it into an
illusion, a mockery, even an insanity. He insisted:

> Unless God is at least as real as my own self . . . how can I pray? If Torah
> is nothing but the national literature of the Jewish people, if the mystery
> of revelation is discarded as superstition, then prayer is hardly more than
> a soliloquy. If God does not have power to speak to us, how should we
> possess the power to speak to Him? . . . The issue of prayer is not prayer;
> the issue of prayer is God. One cannot pray unless he has faith in his own
> ability to accost the infinite, merciful, eternal God.[27]

In his remarks, Heschel knew that he was risking the animosity of his
audience by opposing the mainstream of American Jewish thought. He had
hoped to recreate in America the "Copernican revolution" in theology that
had taken place in Europe between the world wars—a revolution that had
replaced the anthropocentric starting point of modern religious thinking
with one which was theocentric.

At the 1949 meeting of the Rabbinical Assembly, Herberg and Steinberg
had sought to educate and inspire their audience. In 1953, however, Heschel tried to create an atmosphere of confrontation between the new and
the old thinking.[28] The encounter he desired was not forthcoming. Although he had managed to acquire a sympathetic hearing, and even a
devoted following among some members of the younger generation of
rabbis and Jewish intellectuals, his influence on the rabbinic leadership was
almost nil. When Eugene Kohn, an important representative of the naturalist point of view, delivered his paper, he cautiously avoided any real
exchange or encounter with Heschel's point of view. Kohn simply restated
the well-known ideas of Mordecai Kaplan on God and prayer.[29]

In a *Commentary* article describing what had occurred at the meeting,
Fritz Rothschild wrote:

> When the floor was thrown open for discussion, one hoped for a direct
> confrontation of the two positions, for it had been somewhat bewildering
> to hear Dr. Kohn develop at length a position which Dr. Heschel had just

denounced, without making any reference to the previous speaker. This hope was not to be fulfilled.[30]

Immediately after delivering his talk at the Rabbinical Assembly convention in New Jersey, Heschel boarded a plane for Estes Park, Colorado, where he was scheduled to speak at the convention of the Reform movement's Central Conference of American Rabbis. The subject of his talk was "Toward an Understanding of Halacha."[31]

In a recently published article, Albert Plotkin described what happened at the second convention. "Heschel admonished the Conference to return to a Halachic way of life and not to customs and ceremonies." And, as was to be expected, "Heschel's remarks met with great hostility from the Conference."[32]

IV.

In a number of articles which appeared in *Commentary* between 1947 and 1951, Emil Fackenheim established himself as a leading promoter of the cause for a Jewish theology.[33] Ordained a rabbi in 1939 at the *Hochschule für die Wissenschaft des Judentums* in Berlin, he emigrated to Canada where he completed a doctorate in philosophy and acquired a position in the philosophy department of the University of Toronto.

In an autobiographical essay, Fackenheim explained that his first religious writings in America were "occasioned by the experience of a clash between European realities and American Jewish theology."[34] Having experienced firsthand the horrors of Nazi Germany, he was shocked by what he saw as the naive and unrealistic approach of liberal American Judaism. Whereas many German-Jewish thinkers had revised or abandoned their former liberalism after the First World War, American Jewry, in his opinion, was "still arrested in nineteenth-century euphoria," and too heavily influenced by the philosophy of American pragmatism.[35] Thus, like Heschel, Fackenheim considered as intellectually dishonest and religiously blasphemous "the present fashionable combination of disbelief in an existing God with the active perpetuation of a religion as a 'useful' or 'wholesome' illusion."[36]

According to Fackenheim, the question of God is the primary point of contention between religious liberalism and the kind of existentialism expounded by Rosenzweig and Buber, Herberg and Heschel. Whereas the latter attempted to revive the biblical notion of a living and loving God who actively seeks out and enters into dialogue with man, liberalism, Fackenheim insisted, leaves little room "for a God dwelling beyond the world, yet entering into it to seek out man: He is an irrational incursion into a rational universe." Thus, God becomes "a Deistic First Cause or Cosmic Process outside man and unrelated to him, or an idealistic God-idea within him."[37] In Fackenheim's opinion,

> Orthodoxy held fast to the Jewish God, but confined His essential activity to a conveniently remote Biblical and Talmudic past, acting as though the sacred documents of the past could be exempted from modern criticism. Liberalism, for its part, wishing a present God, compromised the Jewish God Himself, now using the terms of Deism, then those of idealism, and in its still surviving forms the terms of a cosmic evolutionism.[38]

Fackenheim, therefore, did his best to propagate the idea of a God-centered Jewish theology in journals and gatherings of the Reform rabbinate. In 1950, for example, he spoke at a meeting of Reform rabbis at Hebrew Union College which was devoted to the subject of the relevancy of Jewish theology to the postwar situation of American Jewry. Together with some of the younger rabbis present at the conference, namely, Eugene Borowitz, Steven Schwarzschild, Jakob Petuchowski, Lou Silberman, and Samuel Karff, Fackenheim argued for both an increased dedication to theology within the movement, and for the restructuring of Reform Judaism along the lines of religious existentialism.

Although, according to Borowitz, Fackenheim's advocacy of existentialism "came as a profound philosophical shock to the assembled rabbis,"[39] the response was generally quite positive. It was decided that an Institute for Reform Jewish Theology be established that would become an official body of the movement's Central Conference of American Rabbis.[40]

As a result of the work done in the institute, Fackenheim and the above-mentioned rabbis began to meet regularly after 1957 at "retreats" in Oconomowok, Wisconsin and elsewhere. It was at one of these meetings in 1963 that they met to coordinate their strategy for the presentation of a common theological front at that year's C.C.A.R. convention.[41] They hoped to be given a sympathetic hearing. However, this was not to be the case. Ben Hamon wrote:

> Any effort at an open-minded examination of an existential approach to Jewish theology was prevented by emotional outbursts, equating Reform Judaism with rationalism and existentialism with Kierkegaard, original sin, total depravity and the blackest Protestantism.[42]

What reportedly took place at the convention was a confrontation between the older and younger generation of rabbis in regard to their respective conceptions of God and theology. According to Ben Hamon, the
older generation could not tolerate the biblical notion of a *living* God, for
"a real God and real commandments would disturb their current social
comfort," and the acceptance of "a serious religiosity would require a revolution." Ben Hamon continued:

> If God had made Himself manifest at the meeting, it was not evident by
> thunder or lightning, by wind, earthquake or fire. But His revolution, we
> are told, is the turning of men, quietly undertaken at the bidding of a
> still small voice. If it was heard amidst the papers and discussions of the
> 1963 CCAR meeting, then something deeply significant may have begun.
> It has happened in less likely places.[43]

V.

The call for the revival of Jewish theology marked a radical break with
the status quo in American Jewish thought. Included in that appeal was an
attempt to justify the theological enterprise itself, a demonstration of the
relevancy of Jewish theology to the immediate postwar situation, and an
argument for a new way of doing theology that was antithetical to the
prevailing outlook in religion. As leading representatives of a new theology,
Herberg, Heschel, and Fackenheim were outsiders, preaching a message
that was foreign to American ears.

In addition, the call for a new theology revealed a generation gap that
existed within the rabbinate. Convinced that the events of the Second World
War had shown religious liberalism to be bankrupt, many of the younger
generation (i.e., the "third generation") responded positively to the call for
a theology which would show the way back to a more traditional picture
of God, man, and the world. The older (i.e., "second") generation, on the
other hand, tended in large part to oppose any talk of a theology which
took as its starting point the rejection of religious liberalism.

In general, the Conservative and Reform movements reacted in similar
fashion to the introduction of the new theology into their ranks. There
were, however, three fundamental differences that ought to be noted.

(1) Although Emil Fackenheim was the first and most prominent
representative of the new theology within the Reform movement, his relationship to the younger Reform theologians was not one of master-to-
disciple, but rather that of friend and colleague.[44] He began to publish his

views in 1947; the younger generation began to publish theirs soon after. Their response was immediate and, to a large extent, collective.

Herberg and Heschel, on the other hand, were charismatic personalities. The younger generation of Conservative thinkers tended to idolize them and saw themselves as their devoted disciples.[45] This appears to have had a negative influence on the quality and quantity of their theological output. In contrast to their Reform counterparts, they were slow to publish their ideas. When they did, their writings often took the form of commentaries on the lives and work of their mentors.[46]

(2) The Reform theologians regarded themselves as a radical, vanguard movement dedicated to the overthrow of the religious liberalism of their teachers and leaders. Regarding their efforts as wholly consistent with the revolutionary tradition of classical Reform, they felt no compunctions about opposing the rabbinical establishment.[47]

Conservative theologians, however, seemed less willing to challenge their former teachers and movement leadership.[48] Instead, they tended at first to rally around Herberg and Heschel, allowing them to lead the struggle against the hegemony of religious liberalism.

(3) Although the Reform leadership generally disapproved of the new theology, they allowed it to have a fair hearing within the movement's institutional bodies and publications. The Institute for the Study of Reform Theology was established in 1950 and major symposia on Jewish theology were conducted at the C.C.A.R. annual conventions in 1952, 1953, 1956, and 1963. The papers delivered at these conferences were published in the *C.C.A.R. Journal,* the *C.C.A.R. Yearbook,* and in the *Hebrew Union College Annual.*[49]

Herberg and Steinberg's appeal at the 1949 convention of the Rabbinical Assembly of America for the revival of theological activity seems to have borne little fruit within official Conservative circles during the succeeding decade. A survey of the *Proceedings of the Rabbinical Assembly of America* indicates a surprising lack of interest in theological issues after 1949. It was not until 1959 that a speaker was invited to read a major paper on the subject of theology per se.[50] In his presentation, David Wolf Silverman declared that it was his intention to follow in the footsteps of Milton Steinberg's 1949 address by providing an updated exposition of current trends in theology. What followed, however, was neither a survey of the achievements of Conservative theologians, nor of American Jewish theology, but rather a lengthy discussion of the development of Protestant theology. Thus there was a serious lack of theological discussion at Rabbinical Assembly conventions, as well as in the pages of the movement's journal, *Conservative Judaism.*[51]

VI.

Joseph Soloveitchik began to introduce the new theology into American Orthodoxy in the mid-1940s. In published articles,[52] in the classroom at Yeshiva University, and in public lectures to graduate students and alumni of that institution, Soloveitchik attacked the status quo in liberal Judaism and expounded a brand of theology that was akin to that which was being taught by Herberg, Fackenheim, and Heschel.[53]

Like Heschel, Soloveitchik was heir to an illustrious family of rabbis; and like Heschel, he combined the best in Eastern European Judaism with that of Western European and American cultures. Soon after having acquired a doctorate in philosophy from the University of Berlin in 1931, Soloveitchik emigrated to the United States where he became the chief rabbi of the city of Boston, and later professor of Talmud and philosophy at Yeshiva University.

Soloveitchik is notorious for his reluctance to publish his writings. Thus, in spite of his reputation as the most important spiritual leader, thinker, and teacher within modern American orthodoxy,[54] his influence as a theologian has until quite recently been limited to what Emanuel Rackman described as "an intimate circle of students whom he teaches and inspires at Yeshiva University and upon the privileged few who see the texts of his lectures."[55]

Rackman, one of the "privileged few," was the first to communicate Soloveitchik's views to a wider audience. He was followed soon after by Jacob Agus and Eugene Borowitz, who on the basis of the essay "Ish Ha'Halakha," helped transmit some knowledge of Soloveitchik's "existentialism" to Conservative and Reform circles.[56]

In a 1952 *Commentary* article, Rackman labelled Soloveitchik's theology existentialist and identified it with the brand of thinking being espoused by Herberg and Heschel. Rackman maintained that like them, "the Rav" condemned as idolatrous the dominant liberal trend in Jewish thought and sought to replace it with an "existentialist" and "metaphysical" approach which stressed "the centrality of God and God's Will over liberal attempts to make man the center of existence and the arbiter of ultimate value." According to Rackman, Soloveitchik, like Herberg and Heschel, strongly opposed the liberal view of religious faith as a means for producing a state of consciousness which William James described as "happy-mindedness."[57]

The introduction of the new theology into Orthodox intellectual circles came about in ways that bear some resemblance to the ways in which it first developed in Reform and Conservative circles. It was, for example, inaugurated in the mid-1940s by a man who, like Heschel and Fackenheim, was a rabbi and philosopher educated in the new thinking in Berlin between the world wars, and who came to represent one of the three major movements in American Judaism. Furthermore, Soloveitchik, like Heschel and Fackenheim, helped educate and inspire a new generation of Jewish theologians. Like their Conservative counterparts, many of whom took Heschel to be their "Rebbe," the younger Orthodox theologians regarded Soloveitchik as their "Rav." And like the former, they were relatively late in publishing their own ideas and reluctant at first to criticize either Soloveitchik or the Orthodox leadership.

If the *inception* of the new theology within American Orthodoxy bears some similarity to that of other movements, it differs from them in regard to its *reception*. There is no evidence to show that Soloveitchik, like Heschel and Fackenheim, found it necessary to storm the citadels of his respective rabbinic establishment with the message of a new theology in hand.[58] As far as is known, Soloveitchik encountered no outward resistance, no opposition, to either his criticism of Orthodox liberalism or his espousal of religious existentialism. One reason for this may be that in spite of their differences with Soloveitchik's brand of theology—dependent as it is on the thought of Buber, Rosenzweig, Kierkegaard, and Barth—many Orthodox Americans would be attracted to its neo-orthodox faith which is traditionalist and supernaturalist. This was especially true prior to the Second World War when religious liberalism had begun to make inroads into Orthodox thought and practice.

Another reason for the absence of opposition to Soloveitchik's theological activities may be the role Soloveitchik occupies in the Orthodox community as its undisputed authority on halakhic matters. In short, no one would dare criticize the Rav. Heschel, Herberg, and Fackenheim were compelled to carry on their struggles primarily from outside of the Conservative and Reform establishments. As head of the Theological Seminary at Yeshiva University since 1941 and chairman of the Halakha Commission of the Rabbinical Council of America since 1952, Soloveitchik is a member of the Orthodox establishment. Consequently, he has been able to introduce his views from within and even from the very top of his movement's leadership. He has not had to venture outside the jurisdiction of Orthodox institutions, forums, and publications to gain a hearing.

4. A DECADE OF CONTROVERSY

I.

Existentialist philosophy, particularly the thought of Franz Rosenzweig and Martin Buber, was scarcely known in North America before 1945.[1] After the war, however, there was a sudden increase of interest in existentialism.[2] Within a very short time, the "new thinking" from Europe bridged the gap between the academy and American cultural life.[3] The only other philosophy to have accomplished this reconciliation in America was the pragmatism of John Dewey. However, while the general public was fascinated by existentialism, most established professional philosophers and theologians abhorred it. William Barrett described the situation at the time:

> The important thing, to repeat, was that here was a philosophy that was able to cross the frontier from the Academy into the world at large. This should have been a welcome sign to professional philosophers that ordinary mankind still could hunger and thirst after philosophy if what they were given to bite down on was something that seemed to have a connection with their lives. Instead, the reception given the new movement by philosophers was anything but cordial. Existentialism was rejected, often without very much scrutiny, as sensationalism or mere "psychologizing," a literary attitude, postwar despair, nihilism, or heaven knows what besides.[4]

In the religious realm, a postwar generation of Jewish and Protestant intellectuals were quick to adopt existentialist philosophy. With Niebuhr and Herberg as their mentors, they came into conflict with an older generation of religious thinkers, most of whom were followers of John Dewey, or of Dewey's style of religious thinking, such as Henry Nelson Weiman and Mordecai Kaplan.

The encounter of the American Jewish community with religious existentialism came about in stages. The community was introduced to the philosophy through the thought of Soren Kierkegaard. Translations of his writings into German before the First World War helped the new trend get its start in Europe. In like fashion, English translations published in England in the 1930s played an important role in the development of Jewish theology in America after the Second World War.[5]

A second exposure of American Jewry to existentialism came by way of Reinhold Niebuhr, the leading representative of religious existentialism in America during the thirties and forties. His influence on Will Herberg and a new generation of Jewish intellectuals sparked a vigorous debate within the Jewish community. His influence within academic circles in general prompted John Dewey and Sidney Hook to denounce religious existentialism in the strongest of terms.[6]

A third stage in the introduction of existentialism coincided with a visit to America in 1951 by Martin Buber, and the appearance by the middle of the decade of a growing body of translations of and literature devoted to the writings of Rosenzweig and Buber.[7] Unfortunately, by the time their work had become available to Jewish audiences, it was already classified as "existentialist," a term employed indiscriminately to group together a wide variety of thinkers, irrespective of the divergences among them. Because little attempt was made at first to differentiate between the views of Herberg, Heschel, Buber, and Rosenzweig, their thought received the same censure aimed at the Protestant existentialism of Kierkegaard and Niebuhr. In *Judaism Without Supernaturalism,* for example, Kaplan declared:

> The Apostle Paul started this cult, which may be called the Religion of Unreason; Tertullian institutionalized it; Kierkegaard revived it after a long period of suspended animation; Barth, Brunner, and Niebuhr have made it fashionable; and some Jewish theologians are now dancing to its tune.[8]

Abba Hillel Silver expressed a similar attitude when, in *Where Judaism Differed,* he pronounced existentialism to be a reformulation of the early Christian doctrine "that man is helpless to save himself." It is, he maintained, "a philosophy grounded in deep pessimism and disillusionment. Its mood is crisis; its idiom death." And such views, "in strange Judaic livery," are to be found in the writings of Buber and Rosenzweig.[9]

This negative attitude prevailed at the country's rabbinical seminaries. Recalling his student days at Hebrew Union College, Eugene Borowitz wrote:

> In those days the academy and the synagogue were quite hostile to Jewish existentialism, so much so that in my six years of study for the rabbinate not one of my philosophy or theology teachers ever mentioned the name of Martin Buber or Franz Rosenzweig. The same was true at the few other schools where those subjects were deemed worthy of inclusion in the curriculum.[10]

Commentary editor Milton Himmelfarb also took note of this situation:

> I am not a follower of Buber, but once, when everybody at one seminary
> was sneering at Buber-*mayses* (a pun on the Yiddish *bobbe-mayeses*, old wives'
> tales), I almost wanted to enlist on Buber's side. They were obviously
> sneering at the theological enterprise itself, and rabbis should know that
> a sneer is no refutation.[11]

Some representatives of liberal Judaism went so far as to denounce, not
only the ideas of the existentialists, but those younger theologians who were
adopting these ideas as their own. Eugene Kohn, in an article describing
"The Menace of Existentialist Religion," accused Jewish thinkers of "misanthropy," for having placed all their faith in a supernatural God, instead
of in man's own natural powers.[12] Referring to the postwar sense of crisis,
he argued that,

> the religious existentialism in vogue in our day, particularly among the
> disillusioned radicals of a few decades ago, instead of encouraging us to
> rally all our mental and spiritual powers for seeking a way out of the
> predicaments of our day, attack the very attempts to do so.[13]

In *Faith for Moderns*, Robert Gordis expressed a similar point of view. In
describing Jewish existentialism, he argued:

> Frequently, its advocates are disillusioned veterans of secular faiths, "tired
> liberals" or disillusioned radicals. In the face of the complexities of modern
> life and the bitter frustrations of totalitarianism, they have lost their ardor
> for the struggle for a better world and have surrendered their confidence
> in man's capacity to conquer the evils of society through their own activity.
> They have, therefore, sought refuge in a God who is "totally other," whose
> kingdom is entirely beyond man's present arena of conflict and defeat.
> Their loss of faith in man seems to them to be the surest foundation for
> their new found faith in God.[14]

There were two "second generation" liberal thinkers who made a genuine
attempt to confront existentialism on a sophisticated, philosophical level:
Samuel Cohon and Milton Steinberg. Trained in philosophy and deeply
committed to the philosopher's quest for truth, both men saw the new
theology as a challenge which could only benefit Jewish intellectual life and
practice.

At the 1953 meeting of the Reform movement's Central Conference of
American Rabbis, Cohon defended the "Jewishness" of Rosenzweig and
Buber's theology, and argued against those who would equate the former

with the so-called irrationalism of Herberg or the alleged pessimism of Barth, Brunner, Tillich, and Niebuhr.[15] Against those who took Buber and Rosenzweig to be opposed to the fundamentals of liberal Judaism, Cohon argued that there was certainly nothing antiliberal in their struggle to re-move "the obstructions that produced the eclipse of God in the minds of modern Jews." Their endeavors are akin to "the classical road of Jewish theology" in stressing the "belief in a personal God" and in seeking "deeper levels of truth and more genuine communion with the Living God."[16]

Milton Steinberg, like Elisha Ben-Abuyah, the hero of his novel *As A Driven Leaf,* sought the truth wherever it could be found, and followed it to wherever it might lead.[17] He made an in-depth study of the new trends in philosophy and theology at a time when his colleagues in the rabbinate found it fashionable to denounce them with vehemence. Without aban-doning his commitment to the principles of religious rationalism, Steinberg responded to the new challenge by re-examining and at times altering his former views, especially regarding God, man, and history.[18] In regard to the standard liberal claim that Judaism had no need of theology and had nothing to learn from the existentialists, he wrote:

> To one doctrine as to the other, the proper Jewish response is that of Rabbi Meir when he said concerning the teaching of his heretic master Elisha Ben Abuyah, "As with a pomegranate, one eats the seeds and throws the rind away."[19]

II.

Will Herberg inspired a great deal of hostility in his liberal critics. Ironi-cally, in condemning his views as "hysterical"[20] and "dogmatic,"[21] they often exhibited these selfsame traits.[22] The consequence of this was unfortunate, for in spite of the myriad of articles written about Herberg's theology there was seldom any real, in-depth analysis of what he was saying—no genuine encounter with his ideas. More often than not, slogans and name-calling took the place of carefully reasoned argument. As Emil Fackenheim as-sessed the situation, "rationalist reactions" to Herberg's theology tended to be "amateurish, not very coherent and certainly failing to do justice to Herberg."[23]

Equating Judaism with rationalism, the defenders of liberal Judaism la-belled Herberg's way of thinking irrationalist, Christian, and, therefore, *un-Jewish.* In articles entitled "The Assault on Reason" and "The Menace of Existentialist Religion," Jakob Kohn condemned Herberg's existentialism for misanthropy.[24] In his article "Escape from Reason," Harold Weisberg called Herberg's theology "a doctrine of despair, an abdication of reason, a return to a shop-worn melange of theological doctrines, advocated by frightened men."[25] Albert Goldstein summed up the sentiments of many when he declared Herberg's version of Judaism a derivative of the "bitterly pessimistic, neurotically negative and decadent gentile philosophies of our time." He described Herberg and his followers as "tired intellectuals, rebels, iconoclasts in their prime," and a "coterie of Johnny-come-latelies, who boomerang into Judaism after ranging long and widely over alien fields and streams remote from Judaism."[26]

A self-acknowledged "Niebuhrian," Herberg was censured by Judd Teller for espousing a "Judaism cross-fertilized with Christian existentialism,"[27] and by Goldstein for a kind which was supposedly derived from "the hysterical aspects of Pauline Christianity."[28] According to Robert Gordis, when Solomon Grayzel was given the task of preparing for publication the manuscript of Herberg's *Judaism and Modern Man,* he was "horrified" to find it so completely Christian and so very un-Jewish. Gordis contends, too, that when Herberg was considered for a post on the editorial board of *Judaism,* there was strong opposition to him on the grounds that "many Jewish readers of Herberg's writings saw in his approach a Jewish version of Christian theology."[29]

It would be wrong to conclude that Herberg's thought met with only negative response. The opposition it engendered was to be found primarily within liberal circles of Reform and Conservative rabbis. On the whole, Orthodox thinkers responded well to his "neo-orthodoxy," as did many important intellectual leaders of the Jewish community.[30] He was held in high esteem, too, by the younger generation of Jewish and non-Jewish university and seminary students. Recalling his days as a student at the Jewish Theological Seminary, Seymour Siegel noted that Herberg's "existentialist brand of Jewish theology struck a resonant chord in the hearts of many, within the Jewish community and beyond, who were searching for roots and inspiration." Siegel continued:

> In those early days, when the naturalistic theology so brilliantly expounded by Professor Mordecai Kaplan was the main intellectual influence in Jewish religious circles, we were fascinated by Herberg's espousal of the orthodox ideas of a supernatural God, Messiah, and Torah, expounded with fervor and yet interpreted in a new way.[31]

Arthur Cohen wrote about the influence of Herberg on his generation:

It is no wonder that when Herberg's essay appeared in January 1947, to be followed in 1951 by *Judaism and Modern Man* (undoubtedly one of the few genuine, synthetic works of Jewish theology written against the background of the American experience), he was warmly embraced (not, to be sure, by the institutional paladins of Jewish life, for they rarely embrace anyone or any teaching not edified by their particular instruction) by a large sector of American-Jewish post-war college students and young adults.[32]

III.

In the 1950s, Heschel's name was increasingly associated with that of Herberg as a leading exponent of what had become known as "the new Jewish theology."[33] Whereas Herberg was criticized for having distorted Judaism by interpreting it according to the irrationalist tenets of Pauline Christianity, Heschel was charged with having falsified it by conceiving of it in the irrationalist terms of Jewish mysticism.

At the time, most liberal Jewish thinkers narrowly defined Judaism as "a religion of reason" and understood Jewish philosophy and theology in terms of either medieval rationalism, German idealism, or American pragmatism. Because Heschel's approach differed from their limited outlook, many of his liberal critics not only rejected the kind of theology he was writing, but even denied that he was writing Jewish theology. Therefore, Trude Weiss-Rosmarin vilified him for being "a tender-minded mystic, poetic ecstatic, expositor of Jewish sentiment."[34] Meir Ben-Horin accused Heschel of promoting a brand of "mysticism," "irrationalism," and "reductionism" that was akin to the "totalitarianism" taught by the Nazis.[35]

Although critical of Heschel and Herberg's frequent disregard for patient argument and systematic presentation, Emil Fackenheim would not tolerate unfair treatment of their views.[36] Thus, in addressing the readers of *Conservative Judaism,* he complained that "one is left speechless by suggestions that Heschel's insistence on a supernatural, self-revealing God must be an import from Christianity. Or that his 'Mysticism' is un-Jewish, reactionary, or calculated to lead us into fascism."[37]

Speaking before a gathering of Reform rabbis, Fackenheim argued that a religion worthy of the name "liberal" should not only tolerate but encourage theological dissent with the hope that truth will emerge from the confrontation of ideas. This was not the case, he maintained, in the way that the new Jewish theology was received within liberal circles. Fackenheim wrote:

What these thinkers should have aroused is passion, thought, self-examination, and, after some time, a reasoned debate which clarified where everyone stood. But remarkably little of this has gone on. Indeed, there does not seem to be a single impressive statement written by anyone in the ranks of liberal Judaism in America, which gives a reasoned account of dissent from any of these thinkers.[38]

The hostility Heschel encountered in the 1950s was caused by a number of factors, two of which are relevant to the present discussion.

First, Heschel's views marked a sharp break with the rationalist tradition in American Jewish thought. He not only rejected the notion that reason can answer the questions posed by faith; he denied that reason had the capacity to ask the kind of questions to which faith is the answer.[39] For liberal thinkers who believed that rationalism is the essence of Judaism, as well as the basis of the American ideals of freedom, democracy, equality, and progress, it was inconceivable that anyone would question what they took to be self-evident.

What made matters even worse was the seemingly incomprehensible way in which Heschel chose to express himself. He translated traditional notions of man, God, and the world into the categories of Kierkegaard and Husserl, Tillich and Barth, Rosenzweig and Buber; and he expounded his philosophy with the boldness of a prophet (which appeared to be arrogant and overbearing), and in the language of mystics and poets (which, for some, seemed pretentious and unintelligible).

The initial reception given to Heschel's thought reflected a polarity between the "second generation" rabbinic leadership, which clung tenaciously to its liberal convictions, and a "third generation" of rabbis and laymen, who were inspired by his personality and teachings.[40]

By the end of the decade, Heschel had acquired great popularity among Jews and Christians. For the former he represented a living embodiment of traditional, biblical faith; for the latter, he was the most important representative of American Judaism and Jewry.[41]

IV.

Reinhold Niebuhr's influence on the development of American Jewish theology is evidenced by the great appreciation for his work expressed, not only by Will Herberg, but by Steinberg, Heschel, Fackenheim, and the younger generation of Jewish theologians. Beginning in the 1940s, Jewish thinkers debated the merits of Niebuhr's views for Judaism. These exchanges helped clarify the issues at stake between the old and the new thinking in religion.

Milton Steinberg was alone among liberal thinkers when, between 1945 and 1950, he wrote articles showing his appreciation for those aspects of Niebuhr's thought he considered relevant for postwar Judaism. For Steinberg, Reinhold Niebuhr was one of the only non-Jews who genuinely understood Judaism. He wrote that Niebuhr "taught us again what our fathers knew and we have refused to credit, a hard grim truth concerning the place and power of evil in man and society." According to Steinberg, the Second World War had disclosed "the depths below the depths of bestiality lurking in the human animal," yet liberal Judaism persisted in its naive faith that despite all evidence to the contrary, man is ultimately good, human progress is inevitable, and man can save himself simply by discovering the right formula or device.[42] Steinberg confessed:

> I was raised a typical modern. I held typically naive and innocent conceptions of the depth and tenacity of evil in man and in society. I think that I have learned from . . . Niebuhr, a salutary lesson in the strength of the Adversary against whom we are wrestling, both within ourselves, in other men, and in the world outside. My utopianism is toned, and realism is born.[43]

A dialectical thinker, Steinberg objected to what he saw as liberalism's one-sided, undialectical view of human nature.[44] Niebuhr helped correct this imbalance in the liberal understanding of the "Hebraic spirit," by stressing the evil as well as the good, the irrational along with the rational in human nature.[45] As a Jew, however, Steinberg would not tolerate what he saw as Niebuhr's over-emphasis of evil. He wrote: "For where we, under the deductions of the *Zeitgeist,* have consistently under-estimated the evil in man, Niebuhr, under the tropism of his tradition, consistently under-estimates the good."[46] Thus, for all his appreciation of Niebuhr, Steinberg could follow him only up to a point.

Heschel and Niebuhr were close personal friends. When asked, therefore, to contribute an article to a *festschrift* dedicated to Niebuhr, Heschel complied with an essay defending the compatibility of Niebuhr's religious realism with the realism of Judaism's prophetic and mystical traditions.[47]

In his essay, Heschel focused on two aspects of Niebuhr's theological realism: his views concerning the existence of the irrational in human life and the human capacity for evil. In regard to the first, Heschel took Niebuhr's position to be wholly consistent with that of Jewish mysticism. Both, Heschel wrote, accept "the final irrationality of the givenness of things";

acknowledge that "tension, contrast, contradictions, characterize all of reality"; and stress that "paradox is an essential way of understanding the world, history, and nature."[48]

More than a decade before the Holocaust became an important issue in Jewish theology, Heschel saw that event as a refutation of the notion that human reason and goodness were ways in which mankind could ultimately save itself. Heschel wrote:

> Dazzled by the splendor of Western civilization, the modern Jew has been prone to forget that the world is unredeemed, and that God is in exile. The present generation which has witnessed the unspeakable horrors committed by man and sponsored by an extremely civilized nation, is beginning to realize how monstrous an illusion it was to substitute faith in man for faith in God.[49]

Heschel believed that by revealing man's capacity for evil and by showing the limitations of his reason,

> Niebuhr not only helps many of his contemporaries to see through their delusions, deceptions, and pretentions; he also succeeds in recovering some of the insights of prophetic thinking that are of tremendous aid in understanding the central issues of existence from a religious perspective.[50]

Heschel's essay appeared in 1956. In that year *Judaism* sponsored a debate between Levi Olan and Emil Fackenheim on Niebuhr's interpretation of the "Hebraic Spirit."[51]

Niebuhr's expressed aim as a Christian theologian was to strengthen what he called the "Hebraic Spirit" of the Christian faith. In "Reinhold Niebuhr and the Hebraic Spirit: A Critical Inquiry," Levi Olan, a staunch supporter of liberal rationalism, criticized Niebuhr and his Jewish followers for having defined the "Hebraic Spirit" in terms of existentialism. Not only were the prophets fundamentally rationalists, he argued, but "Philo, Maimonides, Hermann Cohen, and David Neumark are only four of a great number of Jewish philosophers who welcomed the opportunity to clarify the Hebraic faith by the categories of reason."[52] For Olan, Niebuhr distorted the rationalistic, and therefore the optimistic, character of Judaism by defining it in terms which are wholly alien to it. In Olan's opinion, existentialism is an irrationalistic and pessimistic doctrine, deriving from a theology which is "Pauline, Augustinian, Calvinist, and Reformationist."[53]

In his reply, Fackenheim accused Olan of failing to see that, although he believed himself to be defending the integrity of Judaism against Chris-

tian distortions of it, in actuality Olan was "defending the secularist beliefs
of the Enlightenment against criticisms which are directed against them,
not only by a Kierkegaard and Niebuhr, but also by a Buber and Rosenzweig."[54] Fackenheim held that by expounding the notion that man is a
finite, limited creature in need of God for his redemption, Niebuhr is not
opposing the Hebraic Spirit, only liberal interpretations of it. In Fackenheim's opinion,

> Niebuhr begins with a critique of a concept which has dominated Western
> thinking since the Age of Enlightenment: the concept of unqualified hu-
> man self-sufficiency. According to that concept, man's theoretical reason
> is sufficient to understand human nature and destiny; and his practical
> reason (moral and technical) is sufficient to fulfill its meaning. If this
> concept is sound, then God is superfluous. There may be a God who—
> irrelevantly to human life—presides over the universe; and there may be
> something relevant to human life which is, however, not God but merely
> the human idea of God. But there is no need for a real, existing God who
> can enter into human life.[55]

Like Steinberg and Herberg, Fackenheim believed that Niebuhr's theology
could help American Jews discover the road back to a genuine faith in the
living God of biblical tradition.

The last major controversy over the influence of Niebuhr's existentialism
on Jewish theology took place in 1960 between Jakob Petuchowski, a young
Reform theologian, and Trude Weiss-Rosmarin, the editor of *The Jewish
Spectator.*[56]

Like Levi Olan, Weiss-Rosmarin did not share the antitheological bias of
most liberal thinkers.[57] In fact, she was very much in favor of a theological
revival in the United States. What disturbed her about the development of
the new Jewish theology was its supposed lack of Jewishness. In her opinion,
the new theologians were doing in the Jewish sphere what Niebuhr and
his fellow Protestants were doing in their own. "If a Jewish theological
renaissance is to bloom in this country," she contended, "it must be rooted
in Jewish theological thought. It must base itself on Jewish theologians and
philosophers." Who were these thinkers to be? For Weiss-Rosmarin, they
were Leo Baeck, Hermann Cohen, Mordecai Kaplan, and Franz Rosenzweig, among others.[58]

Anticipating the charge that Jewish theologians were merely following
the apologetic lead of Saadia and Maimonides, Weiss-Rosmarin argued:
"The influence of the neo-Protestant theologians does not plunge students
of philosophy into 'the sea of doubt' as was the case in Saadia's and Maimonides' religious world staggering under the onslaught of Aristotelian

philosophy." American culture, she maintained, is secular. The "thought climate" of American Jewry is not, therefore, affected by Niebuhr, Tillich, and Barth.[59]

In his reply to Weiss-Rosmarin, Petuchowski questioned the appropriateness of her use of Baeck, Cohen, Kaplan, and Rosenzweig as models of authentically Jewish theologians, that is, as persons who addressed themselves exclusively to Jewish problems, and expressed themselves according to norms and in modes of thought derived strictly from Jewish sources. Baeck, Petuchowski maintained, wrote *The Essence of Judaism* in reply to the Protestant theologian, Harnack, "and was accused by Rosenzweig for engaging in apologetics."[60] Cohen's *Religion of Reason* was so very much the product of his German intellectual environment, it "could not have been written in 16th-century Safed or in 19th-century Lubavitch." As for Kaplan, Petuchowski asked, "How much 'original' Judaism would be left in Kaplan if you were to take away his Dewey?" Petuchowski maintained that Rosenzweig was the only theologian mentioned by Weiss-Rosmarin that produced an authentically Jewish theology. It was because of Rosenzweig's success in doing so that, according to Petuchowski, so many of the younger generation of American Jewish theologians were attempting to follow in his footsteps.[61]

In reference to Weiss-Rosmarin's contention that Niebuhr's theology did not account for the "thought climate" in America, Petuchowski pointed out that "any visit to a campus book store at a (secular) American college or university would convince you that the works of the 'neo-Protestants' *are* being read and discussed in academic (and not just theological) circles."[62]

Petuchowski maintained that although an authentically *Jewish* theology "would have to do more than merely put a *yarmulka* and an *arba kanfoth* on Tillich, Barth, and Niebuhr," Jewish theologians would still have to wrestle with religious issues which are common to Protestants and Jews alike living in twentieth century America—issues concerning God, revelation, sin and alienation, the nature of historical progress, and messianic fulfillment. According to Petuchowski, "these may or may not have been burning issues in Sura and Pumbeditha, in Slobodka and in Frankfurt, but they *are* the problems which we face today."[63]

V.

When *A Believing Jew*, a collection of Milton Steinberg's writings, was posthumously published in 1951, Will Herberg expressed his disappointment over the editor's failure to include Steinberg's later theological writings, many of which allegedly showed him to be moving away from a liberal point of view.[64] This situation was remedied in 1960 when Arthur Cohen published these writings in a volume entitled *Anatomy of Faith*.[65] The book appeared to be Cohen's attempt to set the record straight. As such, it created an immediate response on the part of Steinberg's liberal colleagues in the Conservative and Reconstructionist movements.

In a review of the book, Robert Gordis argued that although the articles collected in it indicate "a shift in emphasis" in Steinberg's later thinking, "the basic trajectory of Steinberg's life remained unchanged. He never surrendered the quest for a rational faith." To insinuate otherwise, as Cohen had presummably done, was to "re-create his subject in his own image." Cohen's own theology was strongly influenced by the Christian existentialists, Gordis contended; he wished to see Steinberg as a proponent of the new Jewish theology and thus depicted him as moving in that direction.[66]

Gordis was bent on defending Steinberg's commitment to religious rationalism. Ira Eisenstein, on the other hand, was eager to demonstrate Steinberg's allegiance to Reconstructionism. In a discussion of *Anatomy of Faith* in *Conservative Judaism,* he maintained that although it was no secret that Steinberg had serious differences with Kaplan in regard to "limited areas of theology," there was no evidence to show that "he repudiated the fundamental orientation of Reconstructionism."[67]

In the *Reconstructionist,* Arthur Zuckerman joined the critics of Arthur Cohen by expressing his reservations about the latter's credibility as an editor of Steinberg's writings.[68] Because some of the essays in the collection were derived from badly written, unfinished manuscripts, he implied that Cohen had tampered with Steinberg's words to suit his own outlook.

In replying to his critics, Cohen argued that it was not his intention to create "an apocryphal literature by interpolating secret and alien ideas into the writings of an otherwise good Reconstructionist," for he knew that "it makes Reconstructionists unhappy to read that one of their most notable ones had serious reservations about their theology."[69] Claiming to be uninterested in the interdenominational politics of the rabbis, Cohen stood his ground, maintaining that at the end of his life, Steinberg was undeniably "re-thinking his position" and "turning in a new direction."[70] Cohen maintained:

> It was my impression that the essential disagreement between Milton and Mordecai Kaplan dealt with the crucial question of the nature and providence of God. I cannot, even with a liberal construction of the substance of theology, consider this (as did Eisenstein) a limited area of disagreement. The assumption, as Eisenstein polemicizes, that a change of theo-

logical position requires a new party commitment is obviously naive. For
Milton to disagree with Kaplan over issues of theology did not require
that he rush out of Reconstructionism into either Reform or Orthodoxy.[71]

In the last months of his life, Steinberg planned to give a course on the
thought of Buber and Rosenzweig, both in his synagogue's adult education
program and at the Jewish Theological Seminary.[72] This, together with the
appearance of theologically oriented journals like *Judaism* (1952) and *Tradition* (1958), and the general trend toward existentialism among Jewish
thinkers, might have influenced him to move even further in the direction
of the new theology. Will Herberg certainly thought this was a possibility,
as did Simon Noveck, Steinberg's biographer.[73] There is some evidence to
show, however, that he might just as well have moved in the direction of
the metaphysical theology of Alfred North Whitehead, Charles Hartshorne,
and Edgar Brightman. The issue can only remain a matter of conjecture.[74]

The determination of Steinberg's exact place in this or that theological
camp is unimportant. What is of significance, however, is the relevance of
this controversy as an indication of the changes that were taking place in
the overall situation of Jewish theology at the time. Steinberg was a tran-
sitional figure, living in a period of transition. As such, he played a role in
the revival of Jewish theology in America similar in some ways to that which
Hermann Cohen played in the development of Jewish theology in Europe.
Toward the end of their lives, Cohen and Steinberg began to rethink some
of the fundamental principles of their religious liberalism. While in the
process of doing so, they established personal contact with *ba'alei teshuva*
(Cohen with Rosenzweig; Steinberg with Herberg) who were to become
important initiators of a new Jewish theology which was neo-orthodox and
existentialist in character. In the opinion of some post-World War I Jewish
theologians in Europe (viz., Buber, Rosenzweig, and Samuel Hugo Bergman), Cohen's posthumously published writings pointed the way to a "new
thinking" in religious thought. Similarly, it was the opinion of a number
of post-World War II Jewish thinkers in America (viz., Arthur Cohen, Will
Herberg, Seymour Siegel) that Steinberg's posthumously published writings were moving in the direction of a new kind of religious thought. By
appropriating Cohen and Steinberg as their own, the younger generation,
in Europe and America respectively, sought to win legitimacy for their views
and to gain supremacy over the "old thinking" in religious thought.

Steinberg's later career (1945–50) represented a stage in the transition
from liberalism to existentialism in American Jewish thought. Concluding
a decade of confrontation between proponents of the old and the new
religious thinking, the 1960–61 Steinberg controversy indicated a later

stage in that process. Between 1945 and 1960 the new theologians had devoted themselves largely to negative, polemical concerns. They were busy struggling to win acceptance for the theological enterprise itself, and demonstrating the inadequacy of religious liberalism. Except for the writings of Herberg and Heschel, most of the positive theological work done at this time was exploratory and preparatory, dedicated to the study of new models and trends in philosophy and theology and to outlining the tasks and requirements entailed in writing a modern Jewish theology. The Steinberg controversy marked the transition from a negative to a positive and more constructive stage in the history of American Jewish theology. Having won its case for a new theology, the younger generation was faced with the challenge of proving that it could create a theology of a high order.

5. THE REVIVAL OF THEOLOGY

In 1950 Harold Weisberg wrote: "Everyone, except perhaps a few militant atheists, will admit that there has been a great revival of theology in our day." What kind of theology was it? "A new and vigorous theology," which is "fresh and bold; uncommitted to the grinding of institutional axes." Having "left the shadows of the seminaries," it has quickly emerged as "a formidable challenge to all who deem themselves guardians of Jewish destiny in the United States."[1]

In his 1959 survey of the development of theology during the 1950s, David Wolf Silverman declared: "There can be no mistaking the fact that we are in the midst of a theological renaissance. . . . The stream of theological speculation, which had just begun to widen in 1949, is now in floodtide."[2] Both friends and foes of the new Jewish theology agreed by 1960 that a revival of theological activity had taken place which represented a revolutionary break with the mainstream of American Jewish thought. Weisberg wrote that "there was a general disenchantment with liberal culture and a kind of existential mood among Jewish intellectuals in the years immediately following the war." As a result, "the entire universe of prewar intellectual discourse had been radically transformed." A "counterideology" came about which opposed liberalism and humanism in religion and theology. In time, Weisberg maintained, prewar liberal Jewish thought almost completely disappeared.[3] Identifying postwar Jewish theology with existentialism, Silverman wrote that "it is no longer fashionable to treat existentialism as a passing fashion; as a collection of the aches and pains of the human spirit; as the bubbling over of the pot of human anxiety due to fires of the two world wars and the tensions of an uneasy cold war."[4] Robert Gordis, a staunch opponent of religious existentialism, reluctantly admitted that Heschel, Niebuhr, Rosenzweig, and Buber had made religion "intellectually respectable" for many persons "who decades ago would have regarded all religion with scorn." Gordis complained that "it is symptomatic of our times that the rationalistic thinkers in religion, and particularly the advocates of naturalism and humanism, are at least for the moment in eclipse, while the exponents of the mystical and the ineffable enjoy the greatest prestige."[5]

A study of the literature of the period reveals a number of reasons generally given for this revival of theology and the existentialist form that it took. We shall discuss each of these in this chapter. They are as follows: (1) the emergence of a radically new religious consciousness, (2) the coming-of-age of a "third generation" of American Jewish intellectuals who, imbued with this new consciousness, emerged to write and read a new theology, (3) the establishment of a number of significant Jewish journals which played host to the new theology, (4) the introduction of European trends in philosophy and theology by means of refugee intellectuals living in America, and (5) a revival of Protestant theology in America.

I.

Beginning in the 1950s, philosophers, theologians, and social scientists began to speak of a new consciousness emerging within the younger generation of university students and intellectuals in America. Although described in a variety of ways by different commentators, this new consciousness was said to involve in all its manifestations—political, psychological, sociological, or religious—a desire for transcendence.[6] Purportedly, it was a subjective reflection of objective social changes that were taking place. In Hegelian terms, modernity was said to have reached its *quantitative* limit and self-negation, and was about to give birth to a *qualitatively* different social form which negated and superseded it. Signs of this turning point were already evident within the postwar mood of crisis. What was needed to bring about the new era was a new kind of critical and realistic theory—political or religious—which would furnish the tools for rejecting the old era and its thinking, and provide the inspiration and guidance required for the realization of the new.

According to Jewish and Protestant theologians, the postwar consciousness was transcendentalist and traditionalist in character. Dissatisfied with the ideas and attitudes of modern secularism and secularized religion, which tended to be immanentist and naturalistic, the new generation sought ways of thinking that were compatible with its transcendentalist and supernaturalist outlook. Ideals of transcendence were sought in premodern, traditionalist modes of thinking and belief (biblical, Hasidic, and Reformationist), and in philosophies such as existentialism and phenomenology. Commentators traced the causes of this phenomenon of "return" among Jews and Christians to historical and sociological factors existing in America at the time.

In the 1930s, historical events such as the Depression, the failures of Soviet communism, and the growth of anti-Semitism in America and the world led many Jews to abandon the "false gods" of secular ideology and return to more traditional modes of religious and/or ethnic identification. Ludwig Lewisohn, Haim Greenberg, and Will Herberg were well-known Jewish intellectuals who had accomplished this "return."[7] They were followed in the 1940s by important writers such as Alfred Kazin, Lionel Trilling, Delmore Schwartz, and Clement Greenberg.[8]

The new consciousness was attributed as well to certain sociological factors operating in America. According to "Hansen's Law," while the "first generation" of American immigrants arrived with its religious heritage largely intact, the "second generation" wished to become more modern and American by either abandoning religion altogether or by adopting a kind of religious liberalism which would show how to overcome the conflict between religion and science, tradition and modernity.[9]

According to this sociological principle, the "third generation" possessed a different outlook. Less enamored with modern science and technology and more secure as Americans, it longed to reappropriate for itself a great deal of the traditional heritage of the "first generation."

Herberg used "Hansen's Law" to explain why the "second generation" of American Jews either rejected Judaism altogether or was attracted to a Kaplanist kind of liberal Judaism, and why the "third generation," which reached maturity during and after the Second World War, favored, instead, the more traditionalist outlook of neo-orthodox, religious existentialism.[10]

Anthropocentric in outlook, liberal Judaism allocated to the Divine a rather peripheral role in human affairs. "If we are honest," Eugene Borowitz observed, "we will admit that most modern Jews in the period before Hitler cared little about God and expected almost nothing of God in history." This was the case because the notion of "relying on God was old-fashioned and medieval. We relied on ourselves, on humanity, to a messianic extent."[11]

The postwar generation, on the other hand, possessed a radically different conception of man and God. Its outlook was theocentric, taking the question of God as its ultimate concern. As Herberg noted, the question facing man had become, "What shall we acknowledge as absolute—some man-made god, in fact ourselves writ-large, or the God beyond the abyss, the God who is Lord of all?"[12] For the new generation, the liberal God was the god of the philosophers. It was the consequence of Hellenistic rather than Hebraic thinking. They, in contrast, tried to rediscover the biblical God of the patriarchs and prophets, a living and commanding God: what Steven Schwarzschild called, "the gadfly of the conscience, *the disturber of*

the mental and social peace, the author of an eternal revolution against everything the world represents."[13]

Liberal thinkers generally took a negative view of the new consciousness,
depicting it as an unfortunate aftermath of the war, a malaise that would
soon pass: a failure of nerve. There were others, however, who judged it
to be the result of a deep-felt, innately human need: a spiritual hunger
that has been too long ignored or denied by religious liberalism. These
thinkers believed that, if served by a vitally relevant theology, the new way
of thinking and believing would become more widespread with time.

This latter prediction seems to have been confirmed. The new consciousness and the theological revival it helped foster gained in momentum in
succeeding decades. In the 1960s and 1970s important Jewish and non-
Jewish theologians and philosophers, historians and sociologists analyzed
its further development. In the 1980s, it has shown no signs of abating. In
1982, for example, Paula Hyman, Harold Kushner, and Seymour Siegel
commented on the religious views of American Jews, particularly Jewish
college students. What they said would seem to indicate that little has
changed in this regard since the immediate postwar era. In an interview
published in the *Jewish Week,* Hyman noted that today's students tend to
reject liberal rationalism for it has not provided them with the answers they
seek. She explained that they are suspicious of high technology for they
fear its consequences; they are suspicious, too, of Western civilization because they believe it culminated in the Holocaust. As a result, "they turn
inward for meaning to their own tradition and historic experiences."[14] In
Judaism, Kushner wrote that the "ethnic Judaism" of his beloved teacher
Mordecai Kaplan is no longer able to answer the questions people are now
asking. "They are asking questions about faith, about God, about moral
values. Consensus and folkways are too thin a gruel to satisfy the spiritual
hunger of today's Americans."[15] Seymour Siegel expressed a similar opinion in *Commentary.* He wrote:

> Most surprising is the contemporary fate of naturalism. Wherever there
> is religious fervor among American Jews today, there is a thirst for tran-
> scendence, for mystery. There is a striving—sometimes pathetically
> gauche—to experience God. Even the Columbia University campus,
> where John Dewey taught, does not want Deweyan religion; it prefers the
> Baal Shem Tov. If young Jews cannot find God in Judaism, they will look
> for Him in strange places. Kaplan taught a God who is totally understood.
> It turns out that such a God is irrelevant. God is real and concrete only
> when He is beyond our grasp and understanding—when He is, in the
> words of Kaplan's Seminary colleague, the late Abraham J. Heschel, in-
> effable.[16]

II.

The new, "third generation" consciousness that emerged after the Second World War in America made possible a second condition for the revival of Jewish theology: it influenced the development of a new generation of rabbi-theologians, and provided an audience for theology among Jewish university students for whom the question of God had become a major concern.

Many Jewish theologians in the modern era—Mendelssohn, Cohen, Buber, and Rosenzweig—were not rabbis. This situation changed, however, with the new generation of Jewish theologians in Europe and America. Heschel, Fackenheim, and Soloveitchik were ordained rabbis who possessed doctorates in philosophy from secular universities. And likewise, their followers in America had rabbinic training and advanced degrees in philosophy and religion, and often combined pulpit work with teaching posts at universities and seminaries.[17]

Typical of the new, postmodern consciousness, these theologians interpreted the present era in existentialist terms. Thus, for them the world is unstable, disorderly, and in flux. Reality in general and human existence in particular is too complex, and human logic and language too limited, to allow for the creation of a unified and comprehensive picture of the world or any significant part of it. As religious existentialists, they saw any attempt to write a theological system as arrogance in regard to human reason, dogmatism in the area of religious faith, and blasphemy in regard to God. Fackenheim contended that contemporary "theology cannot wait but must speak whenever the time is ripe, even at the price of fragmentariness. In tranquil times perhaps even theologians can wait. But to the present generation of Jewish theologians apply Hillel's words—"If not now, when?"[18]

Richard Rubenstein and Eugene Borowitz have expressed similar points of view. Rubenstein wrote:

> There was a time, not very long ago, when religious thinkers enjoyed the luxury of a stable institutional framework which allowed them to devote their time to research, study, and writing with few intrusions. Today's theologian enjoys no such calm. His ideas are as likely to be formulated while he is waiting for a jet as in the few moments he can spend undisturbed in his study. Although this work represents a relatively unified approach to the problems considered, it bears the marks of a highly mobile character of the theologian's vocation in contemporary America.[19]

Borowitz wrote:

> Perhaps, then, one should only do theology rather than try to write a theology. That would mean working on individual themes without being concerned too much about what inter-connects them. Not every generation has it in its power to synthesize, and this may be a time in which partial concerns thoughtfully pursued will be more fruitful than a premature effort to relate them one to the other. Approaching Jewish theology by way of significant fragments today may in the more settled situation of another generation make possible a statement of the integrity of Judaism as a whole that is now impractical.[20]

Perhaps the most distinguishing characteristic of these younger theologians was their ecumenical outlook. More secure and self-confident as Jewish-Americans than the previous generation, they were better able to transcend the ideological and institutional factionalism within the Jewish community and to better appreciate the value of the Jewish as well as non-Jewish religious traditions. With the notion of "dialogue" as an integral part of their theological thinking, they set out to "confront" and "encounter" the whole range of the Jewish tradition—the mystical and rationalist, classical, medieval, and modern; as well as the Protestant, Catholic, Buddhist, and Hindu religions.[21]

In his study of Reform Judaism, Gunther Plaut described the new traditionalist or "pietistic-wing" of Reform thinkers as "inward-turned," "ecumenical," and "theological." In contrast to the opposing liberal trend which "includes classicism and humanism and tends toward a separate and definable Reform identity," the former is "less interested in the preservation of distinctive Reform criteria, but rather looks to the *K'lal Yisrael*, stressing the common spiritual and social needs of Jewry." According to Plaut, it puts "emphasis on theology, interests itself in Hasidism, and expresses itself in such directions at retreats, fellowships, and increased attention to adult education."[22]

When Jakob Petuchowski (a Reform rabbi), published *Ever Since Sinai: A Modern View of Torah* in 1961, Shubert Spero, a young Orthodox philosopher and theologian, was so impressed he called upon Orthodox thinkers to take note of the new traditionalist orientation that was emerging within non-Orthodox circles. In Spero's opinion, Petuchowski's adaptation of Rosenzweig's "Third Way," had shown how a common theological groundwork could be worked out between the major Jewish denominations.[23]

Spero's appeal met with a welcome response on the part of David Hartman who, having acquired the aid of I. Meier Segals, organized annual retreats in Canada and later in Israel, where Reform, Conservative, Orthodox, and Christian thinkers could meet on a regular basis and exchange views on theological issues.[24]

Emanuel Rackman described the new generation of Orthodox theologians as comprising the "left wing" of American orthodoxy. They are, in his opinion, "open-minded," "rarely dogmatic," "creative and visionary." Cherishing communication at every level, they are open "to dialogue with the non-Jewish intellegentsia—Christian, Buddhist, and secular."[25]

By its very nature, Jewish theology involves a dialogue between Jewish and non-Jewish cultural traditions. It is important, therefore, that Jewish theologians feel confident and secure, both in their own tradition and in regard to others. In an article entitled "Soloveitchik: On Differing with My Rebbe," Rackman compared Soloveitchik with the younger generation of Orthodox religious thinkers in America. Whereas for Soloveitchik, "there was a clash—a confrontation between two ways of life and modes of thought," namely, the ways of Brisk and Berlin, "for some of his admirers and disciples there was no such clash. They grew up in both cultures simultaneously and the synthesis they sought and achieved was a gradual achievement over a long period of time, virtually from elementary school days through graduate study." According to Rackman, this accounts for the fact that Soloveitchik's followers "are often less timid with regard to the correctness of their views because their sense of security would appear to be greater than his."[26]

Because this new generation believed that "Jewish intellectuals should communicate with each other outside the frame of established institutional lines," and because they maintained "that despite the diversity of commitments, Jewish thought can only be enriched by the exchange of ideas," they conducted retreats for Jewish theologians, Reform, Conservative, and Orthodox. Rackman wrote: "Orthodox youth in the colleges clamor for them as speakers," for they "combine in their outlook and performance the fervor of Hasidism, the critical reason of Mitnagdim, and the ethical sensitivity of the Musar (Ethical) movement."[27]

With the maturation of the "third generation" there came about a radically new religious consciousness, which in turn influenced the development of a new generation of Reform, Conservative, and Orthodox rabbi-theologians. As a result of these conditions, a third condition for the revival of Jewish theology was born: the establishment of Jewish journals that would play host to theological discussion and debate.

III.

The postwar consciousness was not only God-centered and theological; it was also people-oriented and survivalist. Whereas a segment of the Jewish community was concerned primarily with the need for greater theological self-expression, a much larger part of it was devoted to projects that would assure the continued physical and spiritual existence of world Jewry.

After the Second World War, American Jewry was imbued with a strong sense of destiny fostered by the realization that with the catastrophe in Europe, it had, at least for the time being, inherited the responsibility for sustaining the Jewish people and its spiritual heritage. Philanthropic institutions were created for the purpose of resettling refugees, and publications were established dedicated to the regeneration of Jewish intellectual life.[28]

Some of these publications were professional rabbinical journals that reflected the ideologies of the three major denominations within American Judaism. This was true of *Conservative Judaism,* founded in 1945 by the Rabbinical Assembly of America; the *CCAR Journal,* established in 1953 by the Central Conference of American Rabbis; and *Tradition,* begun in 1958 by the Rabbinical Council of America. Others hoped to transcend religious denominationalism by addressing the wider intellectual community. It was with this in mind that *Commentary* was created by the American Jewish Committee in 1945, *Judaism* by the American Jewish Congress in 1952, and *Jewish Heritage* by the B'nai B'rith in 1953.

In her study of the American Jewish Committee, Naomi Cohen wrote that "*Commentary* came to attract Jewish intellectuals who had completely divorced themselves from Jewish commitments during the depression years, and provided them with a means of expression within a Jewish framework."[29] One of these intellectuals was Will Herberg, who published most of his early essays in *Commentary.* Others, many of whom would become editors or writers for the magazine at one time or another (e.g., Elliot Cohen, Nathan Glazer, Irving Kristol, and Norman Podhoretz), shared with Herberg a disillusionment with secular-liberal culture and sought to rediscover the road back to a more meaningful Jewish existence. Although members of the rabbinic leadership sometimes expressed their disapproval of the magazine's policies—criticizing it, for instance, as "cynical," "anticlerical," and "anti-Zionist"—*Commentary* did more perhaps than any other Jewish publication to promote a high level of theological discourse and debate, and to introduce the latter to a readership that included secular and religious, Jewish and Christian intellectuals.[30]

In a 1949 issue of *Commentary*, Will Herberg observed that American Jewry, "the largest Jewish community in the world—numerous, active, prosperous, involved in so many Jewish enterprises—does not possess one single significant journal of Jewish theology."[31] With this in mind, Herberg and Steinberg spoke often of the need for such a journal. At one of these talks, Herberg suggested launching a "Journal of Theological Discussion," and Steinberg recommended A. J. Heschel, Jacob Agus, Robert Gordis, and Jacob Kohn as writers who might be interested in participating in such a venture.[32] In 1952 Gordis and Herberg obtained the support of the American Jewish Congress for the journal, *Judaism*. With Gordis as editor and Herberg on the editorial board, *Judaism* joined *Commentary* as an open forum for the Jewish theological enterprise. Given the general lack of theological discussion at rabbinical seminaries, these journals provided the forum necessary for theologians to test their ideas and exchange their views. They also provided a way for theologians to reach beyond the narrow denominational and professional orientation of the established rabbinical journals.

A fourth condition for the emergence of an American Jewish theology after 1945 was a direct consequence of the Second World War. As a result of the war, American Jewry was introduced to new trends in European philosophy and theology, brought to American shores by emigré scholars and intellectuals from Europe.

IV.

In 1949 Milton Steinberg hailed American Jewry for at long last beginning to produce a significant body of theological literature, and attributed this phenomenon, in part, to the recently arrived emigrés from Germany who had brought with them knowledge of new currents in European thought.[33]

The impact of emigré intellectuals on the cultural life of America after the Second World War was immense, and has been examined in a number of important studies.[34] In all areas of creative endeavor—psychology, sociology, physics, political science, philosophy, theology, and the arts—these newcomers created an atmosphere of intellectual excitement that provided inspiration and guidance to a generation deeply dissatisfied with prevailing forms of American thought and culture. In the fields of philosophy and theology, there were representatives of logical positivism (Carnap, Schlick, Gödel, Tarski, and Feigl), phenomenology (Schuetz and Spiegelberg), neo-

Kantianism (Baeck and Cassirer), neo-Marxism (Marcuse, Horkheimer, Adorno, and Fromm), neo-Orthodox, Protestant theology (Tillich, Rosenstock-Heussy), and Jewish philosophy and theology (Heschel, Soloveitchik, Fackenheim, Berkovits, Glatzer, Atlas, Altmann, Agus). Bertrand Russell taught in America between 1938 and 1944; Alfred North Whitehead from 1924 to 1947. Teilhard de Chardin lived in America for periods of time after the Second World War, as did Emil Brunner.

Important representatives of new trends in European thought arrived in America at a time when many Jewish intellectuals were rejecting religious liberalism and were searching for alternatives to it. These modes of thought appeared not only new, but especially relevant, since they had emerged out of circumstances in Europe after the First World War that paralleled in important ways those that were taking place in America after the Second World War.

The new trends in religious thinking developed out of a synthesis of a number of intellectual schools: phenomenology (especially that of Husserl, Heidegger, and Scheler), existentialism (Kierkegaard principally, but Nietzsche and Dostoevsky as well), and socialism (Marx, young and old; Landauer, Hermann, and Ragaz). In Europe between the world wars, the many manifestations of this new thinking in philosophy, theology, and political thought came about as the result of mutual interaction. The intellectual dialogue that began in Europe among the various proponents of these new modes of thinking was transplanted to American soil in the 1930s and 1940s by refugees from Nazi Germany. This interchange soon engaged the younger generation of American theologians.

A fifth condition for the revival of Jewish theology was the Protestant theological revival that had begun in the United States in the 1930s and reached its peak after 1945.

V.

Liberal Protestantism was considered by many to be dead in Europe after the First World War.[35] At that time in America, however, it had just won its battle with fundamentalism and emerged as the dominant force in the country's leading seminaries, churches, and official organs. Its aim was to reconstruct the essential content of the Christian faith, both philosophically and ideologically, in ways that were compatible with the modern mind.[36]

Philosophically, "the modern mind" was defined in terms of the idealism of Kant, Hegel, and Lotze, refashioned for Americans by Josiah Royce and others; or in terms of the empiricism of James and Dewey, as interpreted in the writings of H. N. Weiman and E. S. Brightman. Ideologically, "modernity" was identified with the social, moral, and political ideals inherent in the "American Dream," and communicated to Americans by immensely popular "evangelical-liberal" preachers such as Harry Emerson Fosdick.[37]

Soon after settling their controversy with fundamentalism, liberal Protestants found themselves challenged by historical events. The Great Depression and First World War forced some to question basic tenets of liberal religion (e.g., its optimistic view of human nature, historical progress, science, and technology), and others to wholly abandon them. Harry Emerson Fosdick chose the former course, Reinhold Niebuhr the latter.

Fosdick was one of the most influential spokesmen for Protestant liberalism, conveying his views on nationwide radio, in bestselling books, as minister both to the Rockefellers and to the congregation that founded New York's famous Riverside Church. There, in 1935, he delivered a sermon that was to have a momentous effect on the history of American religion. Entitled "The Church Must Go beyond Modernism," he railed against liberal religion's excessive preoccupation with rationalism, its naive optimism, sentimentalism, and ethical meliorism, and its watered-down, deistic conception of God. In accommodating itself to a man-centered, secular culture, he argued, it had often lent its support to nationalism, capitalism, and even racism and imperialism. What was called for, Fosdick believed, was a return to a God-centered faith which opposed religion's accommodation to the prevailing bourgeois culture.[38]

Although highly critical of liberal Protestantism, Fosdick did not believe that it ought to be rejected—only that it be critically reappraised and reformed. Thus, after 1935 his position came to be known as "neo-liberalism." Reinhold Niebuhr thought otherwise. Liberal religion, he contended, was bankrupt and had to be replaced by a radical new theology that would supersede both fundamentalism and liberalism. Claiming to have created such a theology, Niebuhr's version of Protestant neo-orthodoxy quickly supplanted religious liberalism as the major force in American Protestantism.[39]

This shift in American Protestantism from liberalism to neo-orthodoxy took place in the 1930s and '40s when Jewish thought was staunchly modernist, liberal, and anti-theological.[40] As a result, when many Jewish intellectuals began to return to traditional, theological modes of thinking, they had nowhere to turn but to the writings of Protestant theologians for answers to their religious questions. Niebuhr's *Moral Man and Immoral Society, Reflections on the End of an Era,* and especially *The Nature and Destiny of Man,* were read with great enthusiasm by rabbinical students. His stress on the tragic and ironic elements in the human condition seemed to be a far more realistic appraisal of what "third generation" Jewish intellectuals were experiencing than the more optimistic religious liberalism against which Niebuhr had reacted.

Would-be theologians who wished to develop a Jewish theology appropriate to the postwar spiritual climate turned, therefore, to Protestantism for inspiration and guidance. This was unfortunate, but understandable, for as Arthur Cohen has written, "American Jewish theology in the forties, as yet unfamiliar with the thought of Franz Rosenzweig and resolutely indifferent to the writings of Martin Buber, had nowhere to turn for the exegesis of the time. Protestant theology afforded the tools for such an exegesis."[41]

This was not, of course, the first time that Jewish theology had developed by interacting with Protestant thought. The revival of Jewish theology in Europe between the world wars was very much the product of a Jewish-Protestant dialogue. This dialogue continued in America with the participation of Heschel, Herberg, Niebuhr, and Tillich, as well as with the students and followers of Heschel, Soloveitchik, and Fackenheim, who devoted themselves enthusiastically throughout the subsequent decades to the study of Christian thought.[42]

By 1960 the new Jewish theology had emerged the victor in its contest with liberal Judaism. Young Reform, Conservative, and Orthodox thinkers were beginning to make their voices heard, and there existed an audience for the new Jewish theology among Jewish and Christian intellectuals. Significant, too, was the fact that Jewish theologians began to rely less on non-Jewish sources and to assimilate to a greater degree the teachings of Rosenzweig and Buber. In the introduction to *Rediscovering Judaism: Reflection on a New Theology*, Arnold Wolf wrote of his generation of American Jewish theologians: "We have all been moved and instructed by the rebirth of Jewish thinking during this century under Rosenzweig and Buber. In a sense, we are only their American continuators."[43]

Almost unknown before 1945, a Jewish theology which was neo-orthodox and existentialist had become by the 1960s the dominant mode of religious thought within the American Jewish community.

6. THE NEW JEWISH THEOLOGY IN OUTLINE

For Seymour Siegel, Will Herberg's *Judaism and Modern Man* was "the first important Jewish book in America to explicate Judaism in the light of the new existentialist thinking."[1] And according to Steven Katz, Herberg has been "after Heschel and Soloveitchik . . . the most influential thinker in American Judaism since the end of World War II."[2]

Herberg never claimed to have written an original theology.[3] Drawing upon the work of a wide range of Jewish and Christian thinkers, and data derived from a variety of disciplines, he had an uncanny gift for synthesizing complicated materials and for presenting them in a highly lucid and well-organized fashion.[4] Lacking what some might consider the depth and originality of Heschel, Fackenheim, and Soloveitchik—as well as their training in philosophy and rabbinics, and their first-hand acquaintance with the new theology as it developed in Europe between the world wars—Herberg possessed what they at first did not. He had an intimate knowledge of a third generation of postwar Americans who were to become the major inspiration of and audience for the new theology.[5] Unencumbered by academic commitments and denominational loyalties, less a scholar and more a journalist and polemicist, Herberg was better able than most to simplify and systematically outline the basic tenets of this complicated and foreign mode of thinking. This he did, preparing the way for others like Heschel, Soloveitchik, Fackenheim, and their followers among a new generation of rabbi-theologians. Therefore, any attempt to understand what Jewish theologians in America consider to be the nature and function of theology must start with the writings of Will Herberg.

I.

Herberg's theological outlook derived from a single, theocentric starting point: the question of God. Maintaining the Niebuhrian principle that to be a self, to be a human being, is to have faith in some absolute or god,

Herberg believed that modern, secular man is, whether he admits it or not, a *homo religiosus:* a man of faith. The question confronting modern man is not *whether,* but *what,* to believe. Herberg wrote: "*What* shall we acknowledge as absolute—some man-made god, in fact ourselves writ large, or the God beyond the abyss, the God who is Lord of all?"[6]

Herberg took the question of God to be essential to our humanity, and interpreted it in biblical terms of sin and repentance. Sin is the turning away from the one true God of the Bible to the false gods of the modern world. Repentance consists in the return to the Living God who is the source and end of our being. Modern man is no less capable of idolatry than biblical man. Relying upon himself alone, carrying the modern principle of human self-sufficiency and autonomy to the extreme, he will come to worship the work of his own hands, mind, or spirit. The result of such idolatry is despair, disillusionment, and demonic self-destruction. This, according to Herberg, was the lesson of two world wars.

Like many Jewish thinkers at the time, Herberg believed that American Jewry was in crisis.[7] His uniqueness lay in his description of the crisis in the theologico-political terminology of Paul Tillich and Reinhold Niebuhr.

The crisis, as Herberg understood it, represented a growing collapse of faith in modern secularism. "Spiritually," he wrote, "the contemporary crisis is a manifestation of the breakdown of secularism, which has eaten deep into the soul of modern man."[8] Viewed historically, "everything modern man has touched has turned to ashes; every achievement of his has been transformed before his eyes into a demonic force of destruction."[9] He has lost his grasp of the meaning of life. He can no longer control the dark, destructive force within himself and society.

Although Herberg's political outlook changed considerably after 1960, he never wavered in his conviction that "the time we are living in is a 'situation of the void'—a period of crisis in which the preservation of the historical stabilities and contingencies against the incursion of the demonic becomes the primary concern and responsibility."[10]

Herberg's appraisal of the modern world was dialectical, combining pessimism with optimism, the notions of "krisis" and "kairos." According to him, postwar Americans were "living in the afterglow of the 'situation of the kairos', to use Tillich's phrase—the time of great expectations."[11] "Kairos" is the dialectical counterpart of "krisis." Most often used to describe a redemptive moment in history in which the divine has broken into the finite world, the Greek word "kairos" is to be found in the New Testament where it designates the "right time," "fulfilled time," or more specifically, the notion that "the kingdom of God is at hand."[12]

Tillich and his kairos school of religious socialism first applied these concepts to the situation in Europe immediately following World War I.[13] Herberg used them to explain what he thought were signs of the dawn of a new era in the United States. In his view, the modern secular stage of historical development was in crisis, that is, in the process of being negated and superseded by a new stage. Contradictions inherent in it, such as those between autonomy and heteronomy, reason and faith, capitalism and communism, had reached their quantitative limit and were giving rise to the promise of a third way: a theonomous culture, open and ready to receive the lordship of the Divine.

Although according to Herberg the "kairos" is the outcome of objective historical factors, its realization is neither automatic nor inevitable. The moment may be pregnant with potential for change. Its realization, however, depends upon subjective, human factors. The "question of the hour," requires human witness and response, consciousness and practice. It depends upon a vanguard generation awakened to its task by means of a critical theology that is "kerygmatic" and prophetic.

II.

Herberg rejected those models of theology which were based primarily upon philosophy and science. In his eyes, they represented abstract system-making enterprises remote from life. What the times required was a theology that proved itself relevant for a mankind caught in the crisis of modernity. Like many of the founders of the new theology in Europe, Herberg was influenced by the Marxist view that an ideology (in this case, theological rather than political) could provide the necessary subjective factor with which the objective historical conditions present in a revolutionary situation could be realized.[14] When he first began to write, Herberg's goal was a theonomous culture and consciousness which would be religious and socialist. Having reached maturity during the Second World War, a "third generation" of American Jewish intellectuals was, in Herberg's opinion, to act as a revolutionary vanguard of the new era.[15] It was the theologian's task to create a radical, prophetic theology which would inspire and guide this generation.

It is important to take note of the significance which Herberg attached to the term "theology." The term had fallen into disuse in liberal nineteenth- and twentieth-century religious thought, replaced by more respectable designations such as "religious philosophy" or "religious thought." This was especially the case in regard to Jewish thought where, in Herberg's opinion,

"theology" was painfully reminiscent of Christian medievalism and the su-
perstitions of the ghetto past.[16] In reviving the term, Herberg was affirming
his traditionalist standpoint. "Theology" was quite fitting for an intellectual
discipline devoted to traditional notions of God, grace, sin, revelation, redemption, covenant, resurrection, a personal messiah, and the like. And
taken in its strictest sense to mean the study of God, "theology" indicated
his ultimate aim: the establishment of an era in which God will become the
center of human thought and practice.

III.

Herberg wanted more than a revival of theology; he wanted a vitally new
kind of theology—one which would deal with the crisis of modernity. Prewar models of religious thinking were, he maintained, inadequate to deal
with it. He argued that, "neither the world catastrophe nor the Jewish
disaster with which it is so inseparably linked has evoked any creative response on the part of present-day Judaism."[17] In similar circumstances after
the First World War, European Jewry produced what promised to be a
renaissance in religious thinking. Given the situation in America after 1945,
Herberg declared: "The age of Buber and Rosenzweig with all its achievement and promise must be recognized as hardly more than an isolated
episode in the almost unrelieved mediocrity of Jewish religious thinking in
recent decades."[18] What is required, he maintained, is a "great theological
reconstruction in the spirit of neo-orthodoxy distant alike from sterile fundamentalism and secularized modernism," a neo-orthodoxy modeled on
the work of Buber and Rosenzweig, Barth and Brunner, Tillich and the
two Niebuhrs.[19]

The neo-orthodoxy Herberg advocated has been called by a number of
names, each emphasizing a different aspect of its multidimensional character. It is known as "dialectical" or "crisis" theology. It has also been dubbed
"biblical," "existentialist," "prophetic," and "question-answer" theology.

In *Judaism and Modern Man*, Herberg held that there were objective historical conditions to show that the present era would be superseded by a
postmodern era, one which will reconcile the contradictions inherent in
traditionalism and modernism in a higher "third way."[20] In *Protestant-
Catholic-Jew*, he turned to sociology to support his contention that there
had emerged in America a postmodern "third generation" of Jews who
were in the process of returning to their religious heritage. These "new
Jews" had a neo-orthodox outlook.

According to Herberg, this outlook reflected a postmodern return to traditional faith, one which superseded orthodoxy and liberalism, traditionalism and modernism in a higher synthesis, or "third way." He wrote that the "outlook of the 'returning' generation is a thirst for the 'metaphysical' . . . a dissatisfaction with the naturalistic and humanistic philosophies that only yesterday were the mark of the 'modern mind'." Although this returning generation is thoroughly modern and American, it often feels itself more spiritually akin to its grandparents than to its parents. "I shall never forget," Herberg wrote, "the dedication which a young man from New York in a select New England college inscribed on his honor thesis: 'To my grandfather, who had the courage to bear witness to the living God in a new world.' Here again, but in a much deeper sense, the 'third generation' is returning to the first."[21]

Although neo-orthodox theology originated in Europe, Herberg believed that it could serve as a model for would-be American Jewish theologians. He believed that the life and thought of Franz Rosenzweig could be especially influential.[22]

IV.

Herberg maintained that, among other things, the new Jewish theology ought to be a "crisis theology." As he interpreted the term "crisis," it means "insecurity, peril, threat of destruction," as well as "judgment, 'turning', decision"; that is, "it also points to the new reality beyond—for the eyes of faith to discern."[23]

Historically, he contended, the modern era is in crisis, nearing its self-negation in a postmodern era. On an individual, existential plane, "crisis" is an essential and therefore inescapable part of authentic religiosity. According to Herberg, it is part of the "permanent crisis of life, an existential crisis which not time nor history can cure."[24] It derives from the "infinite qualitative distinction" that exists between the human and the divine, and the fact that God stands "over and against" man, confronting him in both grace and judgment. Seen as such, "crisis" is a positive factor which points beyond itself to human self-transcendence and a true path to God.[25]

For Herberg, the new Jewish theology had to be a crisis theology for still another reason. He wrote: "Judaism was born out of crisis; Israel is the crisis-people par excellence."[26] This is nowhere more evident than in the modern period, when "the demonic evil and unreason which mankind loosed upon itself in the course of the past generation found in the Jew its first and chosen victim."[27]

V.

Like the prophets of the Bible, the new Jewish theologian must, according to Herberg, speak out against idolatry in all its forms: the errors of organized religion, social injustice, and the like. He should adopt an approach which Herberg characterized as a "God-centered relativism," that is, one which "affirms *God alone* as absolute and therefore insists on the relativity of everything that is not God, of every institution, idea, value, no matter how true or precious."[28] This way, the theologian protects against the corrupting influence of those thought-systems that are based upon commitments at variance with his supreme, overriding allegiance to the Living God. Herberg criticized the absolutization of all man-made cultural products (e.g., communism, psychology, philosophy, religion) as idolatrous, false consciousness. He was aware of the fact that theology, too, could become idolatrous in this sense. A truly "prophetic" theology, he maintained, will be ever on guard against going beyond the limits of human reason, experience, and commitment. Theology is subjective to the extent that it is a "confession of faith." Because reason and language are limited, the theologian must be humble. Herberg wrote: "To stand witness to one's faith and try to communicate a sense of its meaning, power, and relevance: that, it seems to me, is at the bottom all that theology can pretend to do without falling into the delusion that it is speaking 'objectively' from the throne of God."[29]

Furthermore, Herberg argued, modern secularism has blunted our spiritual sensibilities and obscured our vision of the basic facts of life. Liberalism has, for instance, taught an illusory, false optimism about man, God, and the world. It celebrates the status quo and prides itself on showing modern men and women the way to "peace of mind." In contrast, the new theology can help postmodern man adopt a "believing-realism." It will be realistic, Herberg contended, because we will "regain the capacity to see things as they are"; yet it will provide a deep faith that is biblical, "for things we are bound to see once we open our eyes may not be things we want to see."[30]

In their early years, most of the new theologians in Europe and America were socialists or social radicals of one kind or another. They defined their theological position as "prophetic" because it adopted a confrontational ("kerygmatic" rather than "apologetic") stance in regard to religion, culture, and the social order. In addition, they accepted a prophetic vision of a future era in which the Word of God would become the law inherent in all human thought and practice: a truly "theonomous" (Tillich) or "Johannine" (Rosenzweig) age.[31]

Herberg was no exception. At a symposium on Herberg's life and work held at Drew University in 1982, Bernard Anderson called Herberg "a social philosopher with a theological bent," and John Diggins described him as "a radical moralist in search of salvation who became a theologian to better serve his political aims." Politically, Herberg moved from communism to religious socialism, and later in his life he became a political conservative. However, when he wrote *Judaism and Modern Man*, he hoped still that there would be an eventual synthesis of socialism and religion, if not within history, at least beyond it, at the end of days. Early in his career Herberg criticized liberalism from the Left; later, from the Right. Yet he consistently spoke of his religious faith as "prophetic" and therefore "radical," for it took as its starting point the criticism of the status quo in liberal culture, politics, and religion.[32]

VI.

It is because it took God and His revealed Word as central that the new theology was, according to Herberg, a "biblical theology." In contrast with religious liberalism, which allegedly appropriated and controlled God's Word and reduced it to a human level (ethics, science, and philosophy), an authentic biblical theology represents what Barth called a *ministerium Verbi Divini:* an attendance on the divine Word. Thus, God's Word, revealed in the Bible and traditional literature, replaces secular reason as the arbiter in matters of religion, and becomes the source from which theology derives its knowledge, the basis on which it establishes its propositions, and the criterion by which it measures the correctness of its assertions.[33]

Herberg sought to restore the centrality of biblical tradition to contemporary thought without lapsing into fundamentalism and biblicism. Like God, the divine Word is absolute and necessarily transcendent. It cannot, Herberg maintained, be captured by or contained in anything in the world, not even the Bible or biblical tradition. In itself, the Bible is not the Word of God. It can, however, become a vehicle for divine revelation once the individual has learned how to hear and respond to it. Man and God are co-posited in the biblical Word. Revelation depends upon man's subjective appropriation of an objective, divine content. Herberg believed that the task of theology is to help contemporary man rediscover God by means of the Bible.

VII.

Herberg regarded his theology as "dialectical" in two ways. Ontologically it maintained a dialectical view of God and the revelatory relationship that exists between the human and the divine. Epistemologically his theology emphasized the significance of paradox and contradiction for religious thought and language.

In his attempt to revive the dialectical notion of a living, personal God who is both transcendent (Wholly Other) and immanent (Wholly Near), Herberg was faced with the challenge of creating a dialectical theory of religious knowledge that could overcome the problems traditionally associated with such a position.

Herberg stressed what Kierkegaard and Barth called the "infinite qualitative difference" that separates God from man and the world. As absolute Subject, God can never become an Object or an It—a datum for ordinary human knowledge. Although this concept of God constitutes a paradox beyond and against reason, for Herberg it lies "at the heart of Hebraic religion" and is "the irreducible affirmation of biblical faith on which both Judaism and Christianity stand and fall."[34]

Herberg maintained that because revelation often appears to the human intellect as contradictory, paradoxical, and absurd, genuine religious thinking is inherently so. Found in biblical and rabbinic literature, paradox can reflect a higher rationality of its own and point to the truths which ordinary logic cannot comprehend. In his opinion, "anyone who thinks he can formulate a valid Biblical theology without paradox is simply deceiving himself."[35] Furthermore, divine revelation is not only paradoxical, it is dialogical, too. God speaks and man responds. The divine Word is known by means of revelatory events: I-thou encounters which take the form of divine-human dialogue. The transcendent character of God and His Word requires, therefore, a mode of theological discourse that transcends the ordinary, a kind of speech-thinking and storytelling that does justice to the personal and spontaneous nature of genuine dialogue.

VIII.

Herberg was one of the few representatives of the new theology to openly admit that he was an "existentialist." For him, existentialism is "the only approach adequate to the task of making the biblical faith speak out to the man of our time."[36] Thus, what past religious thinkers found relevant in

Platonism and Aristotelianism, twentieth-century thinkers are finding in existentialism.[37]

It was because of his opposition to religious rationalism that Herberg's early critics within the Jewish community characterized his thought as irrational and un-Jewish. Herberg tried to turn the tables on his critics by arguing that it is rationalism, rather than existentialism, which is un-Jewish, because it shares with mysticism and irrationalism a one-sidedness that is inadequate for the task of comprehending the full complexity of the religious situation. In addition, Herberg contended, religious rationalism is idolatrous in its claim that unaided, natural reason can arrive at divine truth.[38]

Religious rationalism is one-sided, in his opinion, because it recognizes only a single model of reason: one which is discursive, systematic, abstract, and objective. This "rationalistic-scholastic" model is not, however, the only one. There is, according to Herberg, a second kind of reason which is "existential-dialectical." In contrast to the former, the latter is "Hebraic" rather than "Hellenistic," "biblical" and not "modern." Deriving from Jerusalem rather than Athens, it is a "faith-thinking" and "life-thinking" that is a viable alternative to the kind of thinking usually associated with the theological enterprise.

Herberg contended that while utilizing discursive reason to its fullest, an existentialist theology will possess "a rational understanding of the limits of rationality."[39] Without losing sight of the proper role of human reason, it will take divine revelation as its final authority. A revelatory rather than natural theology, it will give highest priority to theonomous, "aided-reason"; that is, reason guided by divine revelation which is conveyed in grace and accepted in faith. It will be, therefore, the consequence of divine initiative: of God's search for man.[40]

IX.

Critics of the new Jewish theology argued that Herberg's reliance on Protestant neo-orthodoxy jeopardized the Jewish authenticity of his theological endeavors. It ought to be asked, therefore, what it was, in Herberg's opinion, that made his theology specifically *Jewish*.

Herberg was convinced that Jewish and Protestant thinkers can and often do learn a great deal from each other. This is made possible by the "biblical" and "Hebraic" foundation they share.[41] In saying this, Herberg did not mean to imply that there is no difference between the two. Because divine revelation was, for him, the mutual cooperation of the divine and the human, it comes to us filtered through a particular faith community and tradition. When, for example, neo-orthodox thinkers like Barth, Brunner, Tillich, and Maritain rejected religious liberalism and sought to interpret the Bible anew, they turned to the Reformationists or Thomists for guidance. With the same purpose in mind, Jewish thinkers like Buber and Rosenzweig devoted themselves to the study of Hasidic and rabbinic sources. Herberg did so as well.

In his early writings (1947–1960), Herberg expressed the opinion that to be relevant Jewish theology ought to be built exclusively upon Scripture and the materials of Jewish religious tradition. As such, his thinking was restricted to the task of clarifying biblical revelation in the light of tradition.[42]

In 1960 Herberg reached what he described as a turning point in his thought. In "Historicism as Touchstone," he maintained that he had previously overlooked "the *All Importance of History*."[43] Although existentialism may be a prelude to the correct understanding and appreciation of the Bible, and the Bible is essential to any theology that considers itself Jewish, neither are sufficient elements in an authentically Jewish theology unless they are mediated through the demands of history. For Herberg the question that a living theology must ask is: How does Jewish faith enable us Jews to survive, not only in spite of history, but in and through it?[44]

It is often said that a theologian, as distinguished from a philosopher of religion, works within a particular faith commitment, community, and tradition which he takes as authoritative. While hoping that his message will have universal significance, he writes primarily for the fellow members of his circle of faith. Herberg's theology is dialectical, devoted to concerns which are universally human as well as particularly Jewish. As Arthur Cohen has noted, Herberg was "not only" a Jewish thinker, but saw what he wrote as relevant to all human history.[45] At the same time, however, Herberg's thought was specifically Jewish. Daniel Breslauer contends that Herberg "writes out of a profound sensitivity to the existential particularity of Jews. Jews are different, have a traditional way of their own, and theology has as one of its uses the articulation of Jewish uniqueness."[46]

Like Rosenzweig, Herberg was not a rabbi, nor could he boast of having had a rich background in Jewish thought and practice before deciding to become a theologian. Furthermore, like Rosenzweig, whose "not yet" experimental approach to religious observance he adopted as his own, Herberg strove increasingly to become a more observant Jew and member of the Jewish faith community. In so doing, he saw himself as a Jewish theologian writing a theology which strove to be authentically Jewish.

At the beginning of his career in theology, Herberg listed what he thought were a few of the many urgent needs of the community which required the attention of Jewish theologians. These were (1) a theological analysis of the contemporary crisis of the Jewish people and mankind, (2) an analysis of the inner relationship between Judaism and Christianity, (3) a theology of halakha, (4) a theology of society, (5) an examination of anti-Semitism, and (6) a theology of the liturgical year.[47]

Herberg would have been the first to admit that he did not realize all of the objectives he had set for himself. The following chapter will examine to what extent Abraham Joshua Heschel, Emil Fackenheim, and Joseph Soloveitchik have addressed Herberg's, as well as their own, theological agendas.

7. THE QUESTION OF JEWISH THEOLOGY IN HESCHEL, FACKENHEIM, AND SOLOVEITCHIK

I.

From the beginning of his theological career as a student at the University of Berlin, Heschel based his thought on the conviction that modern man, his thinking and therefore his culture and civilization, are in crisis and in need of redemption.[1] The Second World War, he later maintained, confirmed this conviction for it showed that the modern world's assumptions about humanity—its rationality and capacity for good—were spurious. Heschel wrote: "What we used to sense in our worst fears turned out to have been a utopia compared with what has happened in our days."[2]

For Heschel, modern modes of thinking about God, man, and the world have produced a one-dimensional, half-human being: "callous," "spiritually stunted," "barbaric," and "demonic." Having eliminated the transcendent and the divine from his thinking, modern man has come to experience the absence of God as an objective part of contemporary history. According to Heschel, "Man without God is not human," since "human existence is co-existence with God."[3]

Heschel was convinced that modern man and civilization are in crisis.[4] In regard to the Jewish people in particular, he wrote: "We once lived in a civilized world, rich in trust and expectation. Then we all died, were condemned to dwell in hell. Now we are living in hell. Our present life is our after life."[5]

Heschel was one of the first American Jewish theologians to speak of the theological implications of the Holocaust. Although he never created a "Holocaust theology" or stressed the role of divine revelation in history as did Fackenheim, Heschel believed that neither faith, religion, philosophy, or theology could be the same after Auschwitz and Hiroshima. In *God in Search of Man* he wrote that "in trying to understand Jewish existence a Jewish philosopher must look for agreement with the men of Sinai as well as with the people of Auschwitz."[6] In *Who Is Man?*, Heschel wrote that a new religious thinking "must prove to be relevant not only in the halls of learning, but to inmates of extermination camps and in the sight of the mushroom of nuclear explosion."[7]

In a number of autobiographical statements, Heschel recalled how, when a student in Berlin, he first encountered the conflict between two kinds of thinking: the *modern*, "Greco-German," which prevailed at the university, and the *traditional*, "Biblical" (prophetic, Jewish), he had known as a young Hasid in Warsaw. The nineteenth-century conflict between science and religion, he believed, has been replaced by the controversy between these two models of thinking. And it is not merely the survival of religion that is at stake, but the future of Western civilization.[8]

Although often criticized as an irrationalist, Heschel never tired of stressing the point that Judaism is more than a way of believing and behaving: it is a unique way of thinking with a specific kind of rationality. The task of the theologian and educator, he maintained in a talk given at a gathering of Jewish day school principals, is how to teach young Jews to think in a Jewish way. This is especially difficult, Heschel believed, because "we modern Jews live in a non-Jewish world and think in non-Jewish ways. In fact, we have often overlooked the fact that there is a specific Jewish way of thinking."[9]

For Heschel, the situation was as follows: Western civilization is in crisis because modern modes of thinking have become self-destructive. Because they represent these ways of thinking, modern philosophy, science, and theology cannot overcome the crisis. The situation calls for the creation of a type of Jewish and Christian theology that can re-educate contemporary man in biblical forms of thinking. As a Jewish theologian, Heschel viewed his task as twofold. Given the strong antitheological bias within the Jewish community, he had to demonstrate the significance of the theological enterprise. Then he could justify the introduction of a new Jewish theology.

Heschel labeled as "heresy" the view that Judaism neither has nor needs a theology. According to this view, Judaism is a religion of deeds, not ideas; law and practice, rather than dogma and speculation; external devotion rather than inner spirituality.[10] Significantly, he first encountered this "anti-intellectual" view of Judaism not in the Orthodox communities of Eastern Europe, but in the highly intellectual Jewish community in Berlin. This is understandable, Heschel maintained, because the "heresy" derives primarily from Spinoza and Mendelssohn, who helped make it an integral part of German romanticism and idealism.[11] Heschel wrote:

> In his effort to discredit Judaism, Spinoza advanced the thesis that the
> Bible has nothing to say to the intellect. It was in the spirit of Spinoza

that the slogan was created: Judaism has no theology. As a result, modern Jewish education, with very few exceptions, neglected the field of inquiry into the world of Jewish thought. Jewish thought has been kept a well-guarded secret. The hundreds of books which reflect our people's wrestling with the difficulties of faith, with the profundities of biblical themes, are not even known by name.[12]

Heschel attempted to justify the discipline of Jewish theology by arguing that Judaism is a unique way of thinking as well as behaving, and that the Bible has a coherent philosophical outlook. He took aggada to be "the Hebrew term for theology," and argued that throughout most of Jewish history it shared equal status with halakha. The two cannot, he insisted, stand without each other.[13]

Like Steinberg, Herberg, and others, Heschel maintained that theology is a necessary expression of the inner life of faith and an answer to existential questions posed by the human condition. In the absence of Jewish theology, young Jews often seek and find answers to their theological hunger in non-Jewish theology.

Furthermore, Heschel argued that a genuinely *Jewish* theology must be founded on biblical, prophetic, "Hebraic" ways of thinking. Beginning with Philo and continuing throughout the medieval and modern periods, Jewish thought had been progressively "Hellenized," that is, dominated by thought patterns deriving from Greek rationalist philosophy and science.[14] This process, Heschel maintained, reached its peak in the modern era, when Jewish thought became just another example of "Greco-German" thought.[15]

In distinguishing between two competing types of thinking, the Greek (philosophical, rationalist, idealist) and the Hebraic (biblical, revelatory, existentialist), Heschel was faced with the question of whether a Jewish (biblical) philosophy is possible.[16] There are three ways to deal with this issue. One can maintain that a Jewish theology is possible because both modes of thinking, the Greek and the Hebraic, are in fact identical. Historically, Philo, Maimonides, and Hermann Cohen took this option. Or one can maintain, as Spinoza did, that the two are mutually exclusive. This, however, would make a Jewish theology impossible. Heschel chose a third way. While maintaining the independence of the "Hebraic" (biblical) and the "Hellenistic" (philosophical) dimensions of theology, he believed that the two can coexist within a Jewish theology without the latter compromising its biblical essence. This is possible, because if understood correctly, the Bible can be shown to exhibit a coherent philosophical outlook.[17]

For Heschel, the modern world is in crisis because it is dominated by pagan thinking. As he sees it, the task of a biblical theology is, therefore, "to reconstruct the peculiar nature of biblical thinking and to spell out its divergence from all other types of thinking."[18] Once accomplished, it ought to inspire the world with the biblical images of man and God and "recover the questions for which the Bible is an answer."[19]

Heschel distinguished between two dialectically interdependent types of theology corresponding to two strata or dimensions of religious life. The first is ordinary theology, which inquires into the objective and external, surface aspects of organized religion—its traditional beliefs and dogmas, creeds and doctrines, rituals and institutions. The second is depth theology, which penetrates into the subjective consciousness of the man of faith—those spontaneous and fleeting "acts," "moments," "gropings," and "commitments" that precede "translation" and "objectification" into the subject matter of ordinary theology.[20]

According to Heschel, ordinary theology is an intellectual discipline which is descriptive, normative, discursive, and historical.[21] The product of "Greco-German" thinking, it is often taken to be the only legitimate way of writing theology. Because of its "ineffable" subject matter, depth theology is sometimes considered "irrational" and relegated to the domains of poetry and mysticism. Heschel is a dialectical thinker, insisting on the legitimacy of both types of theology.

Depth theology cannot expect to be as systematic and precise as other forms of theology. However, it can, Heschel argued, "formulate," "point to," and "evoke" appreciation and response to the preconceptual depths of spiritual existence by means of a "vivid, consistent thinking"[22] which combines "intuition with rigorous method."[23] Depth theology ought to precede ordinary theology, for according to Heschel, the former deals with those "ultimate sources of the spiritual life which commonplace thinking never touches."[24] Cut off from these sources, religion—and indeed the whole of modern existence—runs the risk of degeneration and idolatry.

For Heschel, ordinary Jewish theology can help educate non-Jews to the nature and relevance of Jewish teachings and point out where Judaism differs from other faiths. However, it cannot overcome the abyss that separates Judaism and Christianity. On the level of ordinary theology, namely, in the area of doctrines, beliefs, and practices, there can be no basis for theological dialogue between Christians and Jews. Dialogue can take place only on the level of depth theology. At this predoctrinal, pretheological level of faith, all persons experience a common inward sense of sin, guilt, faith, holiness, and commitment: a fear and trembling when confronting

God. It is at this level that Heschel believed he could compare Kotzk with Copenhagen, Rabbi Mendele, and Soren Kierkegaard in *A Passion for Truth*.[25]

In developing his own conception of theology, Heschel explained what he understood to be the nature and function of philosophy in relation to theology. He began by rejecting the identification of philosophy with rationalism. The two are not synonymous, he contended, because rationalism represents only one of many schools of philosophy. Nor can this single school of thought serve as a perennial philosophy.[26] Philosophies come and go in response to the needs of the hour. In Heschel's opinion, the horrors of Auschwitz and Hiroshima have invalidated most prevailing schools of thought, making it necessary to create new ones.[27]

Heschel strongly objected to the widely accepted equation of Judaism with rationalism, insisting that it is "an intellectual evasion of the profound difficulties and paradoxes of Jewish faith, belief, and observance."[28] For Heschel, "religion is not within but beyond the limits of mere reason."[29] Liberal schools of rationalism tend to be anthropocentric, taking as their starting point the human subject and human mind. Heschel's theology is radically theocentric, deriving from Buber and Barth's thesis that God is always Subject, never a mere Object for human thought. Thus, for Heschel, to think and reason about God is not to find Him as an object in our minds, but to find ourselves in Him. The aim of a man of faith is not to know God, but to be known by God. God is not our need, we are His need; He is not our ultimate concern (Tillich), we are His ultimate concern; God is not Wholly Other (Barth), but Wholly Near. The Bible is not man's search for God (liberal religion), but God's search for man.[30]

Heschel's approach had its precedent in the beginnings of the new theology in Europe. The postwar theologians contended that liberal religion distorted religious thinking by reducing theology (Revelation: the Word of God) to rationalist and idealist philosophy (Reason: the Word of Man). Barth and Tillich came to represent divergent attempts at reinstating the identity and centrality of theology, and redefining its place in relation to philosophy in particular and culture in general.

Barth believed that theology, as the carrier of the divine *kerygma,* could retain its mission and integrity only by breaking its ties with philosophy and culture. Tillich represented another approach. He advocated a working partnership between the two, one in which the theologian occupied a place "on the boundary," midway between the questions of philosophy and the answers of theology.[31]

Heschel rejected Barth's position as pagan and adopted a perspective similar to that of Tillich. According to Heschel, philosophy, defined as "the art of asking the right questions," can serve the theologian in a number of ways.[32] It can, for instance, help him locate, formulate, and evoke those ultimate questions for which religious faith is the answer. And it can prepare the mind to surpass itself, reaching into the suprarational realms in which true faith and commitment are to be found. Because, for Heschel, faith derives from insights and intuitions which are prelinguistic and preconceptual, philosophy can help the theologian communicate his subject matter in a coherent, consistent manner. Philosophy can act, too, as a critique of established religious thought and practice, saving it from the tendency to become deceptive, idolatrous, even demonic. As such, Heschel maintained, there ought to be a critical assessment of Judaism from a philosophical point of view, and conversely, a critical evaluation of philosophy from a Jewish point of view. With which school of philosophy ought Judaism to interact? Heschel wrote that historically our present philosophical position is "situated between Athens and Jerusalem." However, this situation is not fixed. "Providence may some day create a situation which would place us between the river Jordan and the river Ganges, and the problem of such an encounter will be different from that which Jewish thought underwent when meeting with Greek philosophy."[33]

II.

Emil Fackenheim has consistently devoted himself to two interrelated issues, one dealing with *faith*—faith in the notion of a traditional Jewish God; and the other with *faith-thinking*—namely, Jewish theology. Fackenheim has asked: Is faith in the God of our ancestors possible in the modern world?[34]—faith in a God conceived of as Supernatural Person, Father, and Judge; the God of Abraham, Isaac, and Jacob?[35] Is a modern Presence of this ancient God possible today?[36] Or, is man radically alone, closed to the incursion of the Divine?[37] Fackenheim asks: If, indeed, the Jewish God can once again live in present as well as past history, "How shall we live with God after Auschwitz? How without Him?"[38]

Because Fackenheim understands Jewish theology to be a synthesis of two kinds of thinking, the philosophical and the religious, he is compelled to ask: How is it possible to have a discipline that claims to attain universal validity (for what is true, is true for everyone) and yet is particularly Jewish (assigning a special position to Jewish tradition)?[39] How is it possible to join together modern philosophy's dedication to the principles of reason, autonomy, and objective detachment with religion's commitment to revelation, heteronomy, and subjective faith commitment? If, indeed, there can be a modern Jewish theology, what must it be like, and how can it bear witness to and champion the cause of a Jewish God in a post-Holocaust world?[40]

Fackenheim was born in Halle, Germany in 1916 and was ordained at the prestigious *Hochschule für die Wissenschaft des Judentums* in Berlin in 1939. Early in his career, he already considered himself a follower of neo-ortho-dox theologians Buber and Rosenzweig, Barth, Tillich, and Niebuhr. By neo-orthodox he meant a theological position that was supernaturalist and existentialist. He was especially critical of religious liberalism, which in his opinion had "sucked the life out of Judaism and transformed its insights into platitudes."[41] When he arrived in North America in 1940, Fackenheim encountered within Jewish intellectual life what he took to be a pitifully outdated religious liberalism which was Jewish in name only. This was especially true in regard to its conception of God.[42]

Theology is by definition the "science," "study," or "discourse" about God. If a theology is to be genuine, Fackenheim maintained, not just any God will suffice. While philosophy *qua* philosophy can at best only affirm the possibility of divine revelation, theology *qua* theology must categorically affirm its actuality. To do so presupposes a prior commitment to a personal, supernatural, traditionally Jewish God who can and does reveal His Word to mankind. In Fackenheim's opinion, a genuinely *Jewish* theology must accept Jewish tradition as divinely revealed and therefore authoritative for Jewish thought. Fackenheim did not believe that liberal Jewish thought in America met these requirements. First, it took Reason (philosophy, sociology, psychology, human culture) rather than Revelation (Torah, Tradition) as its authoritative starting point. Like Heschel and Soloveitchik, Fackenheim believed that Maimonides, the prime example of Jewish rationalist philosophy, was an authentic *Jewish* theologian and philosopher because, in contrast to modern liberal thinkers, he took divine revelation as his ultimate authority. He did so, for example, when he allowed for miraculous interruptions into the order of nature, of which divine revelation was considered by him to be the most important.[43]

Liberal Jewish thought was *un-Jewish,* according to Fackenheim, in still another way: it had replaced the biblical notion of God with an abstract, impersonal Principle, Ideal, Idea, Cause, or Process, and identified revelation with reason and inspiration. As a result, the Bible lost its authority and was reduced to the level of other "Great Books" in Western civilization, all of which represented an advanced stage in the evolution of human reason and morality.

While prewar American Jewish thought was judged by Fackenheim to be lacking those notions essential to be authentic Jewish theology, its alleged lack of "system" and "argumentation" disqualified it as true theology.

Fackenheim is a religious existentialist. Like most post-Hegelian thinkers (viz., the logical positivists, language analysts, pragmatists, and phenomenologists), most existentialists reject as futile any attempt at system-building in philosophy and theology. Thus, Fackenheim argues that Jewish spiritual existence in the modern world is fragmentary, contradictory, and turbulent, and doubts therefore "whether even the most gifted theologian could produce a systematic theology in all details."[44] It is probably for this reason that Fackenheim prefers to publish collections of essays and lectures. His only book, as such, is *To Mend the World.* And, to indicate that he has not written completed theological systems, he has entitled his books "Outlines," "Reflections," "Foundations," "Essays," and "A Preface."[45]

In *To Mend the World,* Fackenheim goes even further by insisting that Rosenzweig's *Star of Redemption* is "not only the most recent but also the last system, not only within the sphere of Jewish thought but also beyond it." The only thing that remains of system when systems have come to an end is, for Fackenheim, "the systematic labor of thought."[46] Convinced that to think is to think systematically, and that a theology devoid of system is a contradiction in terms, he believes that at least fragments of a system can and ought to be produced.[47] It is only by keeping the ideals of consistency and coherence in mind that the theologian can reach a level of debate by which opposing schools of thought can argue their respective cases and communicate with each other.[48]

If, for Fackenheim, a correct understanding of "system" is important, a like understanding of "essence" is as well.[49] In dealing with both of these notions, Fackenheim tries to steer a course midway between the absolutism of extreme idealism and the nihilism of an extreme existentialism. His solution lies in redefining "essence" as "framework" or "structure," that is, as a dynamic and open whole that can absorb novel historical events and respond to others by means of internal restructuring.[50]

For Fackenheim, the "framework" of Judaism, and, therefore, of an authentically Jewish theology, derives from Midrash: "the profoundest and most authentic theology ever produced within Judaism."[51] It is, he maintains, "written not in the form of a system—final, air-tight and fully spelled-out—but rather in the merely fragmentary and suggestive form of story and parable."[52] As Fackenheim understands it, the "midrashic framework" is not a fixed and eternal essence, but an open whole with a logic all its own. It is dialectical, holding fast to contradictory affirmations, and aggadic, expressing itself symbolically and anthropomorphically.

Fackenheim is attempting here to avoid idealist notions of System, Essence, and History, while retaining important aspects of each. With this in mind, he defines normative Judaism (and, therefore, *Jewish* theology) as "midrashic," and contends that there is a midrashic "framework" or "structure" which is a fragmentary, contradictory yet consistent whole, held together by faith and commitment. Before 1967, Fackenheim held an absolutist view, maintaining that this midrashic structure was "closed" and therefore immune to the challenges of history. After the 1967 Arab-Israeli War, he began to understand the structure of Jewish thought as an "open whole," exposed and vulnerable to historical change.[53]

For Fackenheim, Jewish theology is midrashic, both in logic and language. In regard to God, he writes, "Man must speak symbolically; or (if we wish) anthropomorphically; for he speaks from his finite situation." Although anthropormorphic language is not absolute truth, neither is it falsehood: "It is the truth about the God-man relation as it appears from the standpoint of man; and that relation is itself a reality. How it appears from the standpoint of God, man cannot fathom, nor is it his business to fathom it."[54]

In articles published between 1952 and 1963, Fackenheim explored the theological relevance of objective and subjective forms of thinking. In reviews of Heschel's *Man is Not Alone* and *God in Search of Man,* Fackenheim maintained that there are at least two kinds of thinking found in these works: two methodologies and tasks for the Jewish theologian.[55] The first is "descriptive" or "first-order" thinking.[56] It represents a phenomenological description of religious truths, immediately apprehended by the theologian as a man of faith. Based on the latter's experience of "radical amazement" and enthrallment with "the Ineffable," he expresses these "moments of faith" in a poetic and aphoristic style, which is, according to Fackenheim, authentically midrashic and Jewish.[57]

Fackenheim claimed to have discovered another type of thinking in Heschel's writings—the "argumentative" or "second-order" kind.[58] It involves the demonstration, justification, and definition of those religious truths expressed in "first-order" thinking.

In his article "The Revealed Morality of Judaism and Modern Thought," Fackenheim spoke of these ways of thinking in terms of philosophy and religion, reason and revelation, detached and committed, objective and subjective modes of thought—and argued that the very possibility of writing a modern Jewish theology depended on a correlation of the two. This can be accomplished, he argued, by "a sympathetic phenomenological re-enactment," in which philosophical detachment is combined with the sympathetic understanding of truths accepted on the basis of faith.[59]

Fackenheim shares with other neo-orthodox thinkers an ambivalent attitude toward the philosophical enterprise as it is ordinarily conceived. His dilemma is this: he believes that Jewish theology ought to be an expression of consistent, coherent, and systematic (i.e., "philosophical") thinking about Jewish faith and existence. As generally conceived from Plato to Hegel, philosophy deals primarily with subject matter which is universal and objective. However, according to Fackenheim, Jewish faith and existence is highly subjective and unique. An authentic Jewish theology must therefore unite the subjective and objective, I-Thou and I-It ways of knowing. Abstract idealism will not do. Jewish theologians, "if needing the language of philosophy at all, need a language of concreteness which speaks to us of human death and finitude, of the actual world and of existential decision."[60] In Fackenheim's opinion, the only kind of philosophy compatible with Jewish theology is existentialism. Although he expresses reservations about existentialism's ability to do full justice to the absolute uniqueness of Jewish existence after the Holocaust, Fackenheim implies that its mode of "faith thinking" comes closest to solving the problem of combining the universal and particular, objective and subjective, rational and supra-rational realms of human thought.

In 1967, Fackenheim developed further his solution to the problem of objective and subjective thinking in theology. In *God's Presence in History*, he distinguished between "religious immediacy" (subjective, faith-thinking) and "critical reflection" (objective, secular-thinking), and, borrowing a concept from Kierkegaard, spoke about the correlation of the two as "immediacy after reflection."[61]

Fackenheim's solution involved a "third way" beyond the extremes of objectivity and subjectivity. He reconciled the two by claiming that they serve as necessary stages in contemporary theological thinking. As a man of faith, he wrote, the Jewish theologian stands within the midrashic framework and is engaged in a mode of thinking founded on "religious immediacy." As a modern secular man, on the other hand, today's Jewish theologian must also step outside the framework of "religious immediacy," and from a perspective of detached "critical reflection," call into question the ontological and epistemological foundations of midrashic faith. Once this is accomplished, Fackenheim argued, the Jewish theologian can and ought to perform an act of intellectual *teshuva* in which he returns to a position of "religious immediacy after reflection." Having risked the loss of faith, he stubbornly and heroically recommits himself to and re-enters the framework of Jewish faith.

Fackenheim is a crisis theologian. His whole theological enterprise is based on the conviction that Jewish faith, and therefore Jewish thought, is in crisis in the modern world—called into question first by the Emancipation, and after the Second World War, by the Holocaust. The Emancipation brought Judaism into confrontation with a kind of secular thinking unprecedented for its radicalism; the Holocaust, with a historical event unprecedented in human history. The former threatened Jewish thought from without, the latter from within.[62]

Fackenheim's early theological writings (1947–67) were ahistorical, dealing primarily with the "crisis of modernity," namely, the confrontation between traditional Jewish and modern, secular modes of thought. He wrote as though Jewish faith was immune to the accidents of history. He saw the Holocaust as an expression of human evil and he treated it abstractly in terms of the philosophical "problem of evil." In 1967 a change took place in his outlook—one so drastic that he later looked back at this period "with religious and theological guilt and repentance."[63] The immediate catalyst for his change of mind was the 1967 Arab-Israeli War. Fackenheim realized that if the Israelis had lost the war, world Jewry would have faced the possibility of a second Holocaust. In dramatic fashion, therefore, the war brought the Holocaust to his attention, and with it, questions concerning the *theological* significance of Jewish history.[64]

Modernity calls into question not only the midrashic *form,* but also the existential *content* of Jewish thought. For Fackenheim, this content is grounded in Judaism's faith in a living God who enters into human history and relates to Israel as a saving and commanding Presence. In its most radical form, modern secular thought denies the possibility of such divine-human relationship. All claims concerning human openness to God and all talk about the objective content of religious experience are rejected in principle as epistemologically unjustifiable.

Fackenheim argued that the Holocaust threatens faith in the possibility and actuality of the divine-human relationship, not from the side of man (who due to his secular outlook may have already closed himself to the divine), but from the side of God who, it can be argued, failed to intervene in human history when He was needed most. Whereas modern secularism may have caused the "eclipse" of God in contemporary thought, the Holocaust may spell the "death" of God and mark an end to Jewish theology. Fackenheim's own theological enterprise is especially vulnerable in this regard, because it is based on the thesis that authentic Jewish theology stands or falls with its commitment to a living God who reveals His will in human history.

Fackenheim's theological perspective is neo-orthodox and existentialist, combining his understanding of Jewish faith as essentially "midrashic" with categories drawn from Buber, Rosenzweig, Kierkegaard, and Niebuhr. For Fackenheim, therefore, "the analysis of the human condition constitutes the necessary prolegomenon for all modern Jewish, and indeed all modern theology."[65] As a person, the Jewish theologian is part of the human condition; as a Jew, he is situated within a particular faith community. Unlike the philosopher and scientist, his personal faith experience and commitment enters into his work. The theologian, according to Fackenheim, must be both humble and modest in his claims to truth since by its very nature, theological truth joins together the subjective and objective, finite and infinite, the human and the divine.

This personal, subjective dimension gives to neo-orthodoxy its expressionistic and confessional character, and in Fackenheim's opinion, justifies the theologian's occasional use of an autobiographical form of discourse. He has written: "In writing autobiographically, the theologian puts, so to speak, his cards on the table. The reader can judge for himself whether the writer's experience has affected the universality of his conclusions, and if he finds this to be the case, he can discount them."[66]

In Fackenheim's opinion, most nineteenth- and twentieth-century religious thought responded to the challenge of modernity by either rejection and retreat or compromise and surrender. Orthodoxy, along with mysticism and romanticism, took the former path, liberalism the latter. Neo-orthodoxy, he maintains, represents a third alternative: the way of radical encounter and confrontation.[67]

Fackenheim contends that while Hermann Cohen and Franz Rosenzweig were among the first Jewish thinkers to respond radically to modernity, they did not go far enough. And whereas Buber's philosophy of dialogue may suffice to meet the challenge of secularism, it is not radical enough to deal with the Holocaust.[68] To be sufficiently radical for today, a Jewish theology must, he argues, apply the dialectical principles of mutual "self-exposure" and "encounter" to all dimensions of *thought*—secular, Jewish, and Christian; and *history*—especially the Holocaust and the reborn Jewish state. In a post-Holocaust world, Jewish theology must wrestle, struggle, and contend with God in increasingly radical ways. Fackenheim writes: "At one time the great question may have been how to make Judaism modern. Today the great question is how to save it as Judaism."[69] How is the latter to be accomplished? The theologian, as a man of faith, must make what Fackenheim calls "a radical turning—a turning to the ancient God in the very midst of modernity."[70] In saying this, Fackenheim is not necessarily calling for a return to orthodox practice, but rather to a traditional faith in a traditionally Jewish God. Moreover, the return he envisions is one that will take place *in the midst of* modernity. Uncompromising in his faith commitment, the theologian goes out to do battle, contending with God, man, and the world.

III.

In writing Jewish theology in America, Soloveitchik shares with Heschel and Fackenheim the task of demonstrating the significance of the theological enterprise for Judaism. Given his reputation in the modern Orthodox community, Soloveitchik is in a position to defend theology as few others can.

Like Heschel, Soloveitchik rejected as "simplistic and erroneous" the argument that Judaism has no need for theology since it is a purely rational, this-worldy faith, devoid of binding dogmas and concerned solely with deeds, practice, halakha.[71] As himself a paradigm of the "man of halakha," Soloveitchik is able to lend legitimacy to the discipline of theology by personal example, that is, by combining halakha and aggada, law and theology, in his teaching, lecturing, and writing.

Heschel and Fackenheim have written clear and sustained accounts of what they mean by Jewish theology and their motives for writing it. Soloveitchik has not done the same. At first glance, it would appear that he had done so in 1944 when he wrote *The Halakhic Mind,* a work that was not published until 1986. However, in contrast to his other major works, Soloveitchik does not speak in it of *theology* but rather of the *philosophy of religion,* and devotes himself primarily to the task of demonstrating the methodological autonomy of the latter discipline. He does not indicate whether he will himself adopt the methodology of which he speaks; nor for that matter is it clear that he has done so in his theological writings published since 1944.[72]

The clearest and most sustained expression of Soloveitchik's theological intentions and methodology are to be found in "The Lonely Man of Faith."[73] He had a twofold aim in writing this essay. He saw it in regard to himself as a *therapeutic* exercise which was expressive and confessional. For others, he hoped it would be *informative,* i.e., descriptive and educational.

In "The Lonely Man of Faith," Soloveitchik argued that the faith experience involves loneliness and conflict, crisis and despair. As a consequence, Soloveitchik, as a man of faith, had "a burning thirst for communication,"[74] an overpowering need "to speak," "to confide," "to confess"—"to tell his tale of a personal dilemma."[75] Having joined the covenantal faith community as a *homo absconditus*, the man of faith seeks to become a *homo revelatus* by "objectifying," "crystalizing," "interpreting," and "converting" his inner life into "external facticity."[76] Expressing himself in theological terms is a "therapeutic," "cathartic," and "redemptive" act, for "there is a redemptive quality for an agitated mind in the spoken word and a tormented soul finds peace in confessing."[77] Understood in this way, theology becomes an autobiographical, confessional endeavor. It expresses the unique, existential situation of the man of faith in the modern world.

Soloveitchik's second purpose in writing "The Lonely Man of Faith" was to be informative, to "define the great dilemma confronting the contemporary man of faith" so that he will comprehend his "place and role within the scheme of events and things willed and approved by God."[78]

Having acknowledged his motives for writing the article, Soloveitchik next described the nature of the methodology he would be employing. In contrast to ordinary types of theology, he said that he would not be concerned with constructing a systematic and consistent, detached and impersonal theory which claimed to be definitive and universally true. Instead, Soloveitchik wanted to present an *interpretation* of his "spiritual perceptions and emotions in modern theologico-philosophical categories."[79] Taking himself and his specific situation as a lonely man of faith to be his starting point and subject matter, his endeavors would be "modest" and "subjective."[80] His intention was not to demonstrate the truth of what he was saying in the ordinary sense, but to move his audience, to appear "relevant," and to find some "response" in their "hearts."[81]

Soloveitchik went on to distinguish between two antithetical personality types and their respective communities: the man of faith and his "covenantal-existential Halakhic community," and the man of religion and his "modern," "majestic," "secular" community.[82] Since the kind of in-depth sharing and confessing Soloveitchik identified with his theological enterprise can exist only within the former community, it follows that he was addressing his theological works only to members of his own Orthodox (covenantal, halakhic) faith community. Thus, Silberman wrote that "Soloveitchik is in fact eschewing apologetic theology in favor of dogmatics, as Barth too had done and as Rosenzweig had recommended—a confessional theology of a very high order." In Silberman's opinion, "it is spoken to those who already stand within the covenantal faith community, and can be understood in its intellectual seriousness only by them."[83]

There is *implicit* in "The Lonely Man of Faith" a second type of theology, directed to another type of audience. Whereas in addressing his own faith community Soloveitchik wrote of "interpreting" and "sharing" his experiences, he spoke of "translating" and "delivering" the *kerygma* of faith to the modern man of religion and culture.[84]

What seems to emerge from his discussion are two types of theology resembling in important respects the distinction Heschel and Fackenheim made between a first-order, depth theology and a second-order, ordinary theology.[85] And, like them, Soloveitchik understood the role of the theologian in terms of the alleged "crisis of modernity."[86]

For Soloveitchik, modernity is in crisis and theological "interpretation" and "translation" are means by which the crisis can be defined, comprehended, and to some extent overcome. The term "modern" was not ordinarily used by Soloveitchik as a synonym for "contemporary." Instead, it represented a specific kind of rationality and *weltanschauung*. Conceived in the Enlightenment and expressed in German idealism, modern man is a majestic, Promethean figure; an autonomous creator and ruler over religion and culture, history and society.[87]

In "The Man of Halakha" Soloveitchick described modern man and his rationality in terms of Kantian and neo-Kantian categories. In "The Lonely Man of Faith," he expanded this to include the secular-functional rationality of twentieth-century America.[88] In both essays he assigned to modern secularism the highest of legitimacy: divine sanction. Potentially, modern man has the capacity to fulfill his divine mandate as co-creator with God. Actually, however, he has become "idolatrous," even "demonic"; his divinely ordained will to power and dominion, dignity, and status have gone awry. Commanded to live a dialectical life of faith and majesty, he stubbornly rejects the second and equally essential faith dimension of his humanity.[89]

Paul Tillich is credited with having revived the notion of "the demonic," and for having shown its dialectical relationship to such notions as "modern man" and "modern creativity."[90] Important elements of Tillich's definition of these terms were employed by Soloveitchik in "The Lonely Man of Faith" to describe modern "Majestic Man" (or, "Adam I"). Thus, Soloveitchik maintained that "Majestic Man" is "aggressive, bold, and victory minded. His motto is success, triumph over the cosmic forces. He engages in creative work, trying to imitate his Maker." This positive trait is accompanied by one which is negative. "Majestic Adam has developed a demonic quality: laying claim to unlimited power—alas to infinity itself. His pride is almost boundless, his imagination arrogant, and he aspires to complete and absolute control of everything."[91]

This was Soloveitchik's scenario. It is a biblical drama of sin and idolatry, repentence and hope. It is the theologian as prophet who brings to modern man the redeeming *kerygma* of faith.[92]

Soloveitchik's man of faith is commanded by God to "translate" and "deliver" the *"kerygma* of faith" to the modern "man of culture," *"homo religiosus."*[93] Use of this terminology suggests a well-known theological debate that began in Germany during Soloveitchik's student days at the University of Berlin.

For Karl Barth, the father of dialectical, crisis theology, religious liberalism was idolatrous. Subordinating God's Word to human culture, liberals had allegedly produced a compromised, apologetic theology which had lost its power to redeem. God and man, revelation and reason, faith and religion, theology and philosophy are *qualitatively* distinct and ought therefore to be kept apart. According to Barth, the theologian's task is a prophetic one: to liberate theology from subservience to philosophy and culture so that it can better deliver the Word of God by casting it in judgment over and against the modern world.[94]

Tillich, Brunner, and Bultmann eventually came to differ with Barth by upholding the significance of "polemical apologetics" (Brunner), "theological translation" (Bultmann), and the close "correlation" (Tillich) of religious faith with secular culture (i.e., philosophy, psychology, sociology, art, language). Tillich saw himself as a theologian of culture, mediating between the questions of culture (reason) and the answers of faith (revelation).[95]

Although indebted to Barth in a number of respects,[96] Soloveitchik was clearly in the camp of Tillich, Brunner, and Bultmann in regard to the notion of theological translation. His position was, however, uniquely his own—and problematic, at that.

Having defined the faith experience as "mysterious," "numinal," "aboriginal," and "unique,"[97] Soloveitchik acknowledged the almost insurmountable difficulties involved in translating it into the general categories of human language and thought.[98] The disparity between the message and its medium seemed too great. More specifically, he realized the obstacles involved in converting this message into the particular "foreign language" and "cultural vernacular" of modern, secular man.[99] For Soloveitchik, the *"kerygma* of original faith in all its singularity and pristine purity" was incompatible with "the fundamental credo of a utilitarian society."[100]

If we assume the Kantian principle that *ought* implies *can,* and infer that because God has commanded it, the man of faith can translate his message, two questions remain. To what extent does the translated faith *kerygma* retain its power; and once translated, is the man of faith qualified for the possibly Sisyphean task of delivering it?[101]

Soloveitchik appeared to have reasons for his optimism, guarded as it is. First, he insisted that there is a certain "parallelism," or correlation that exists between religious faith and modern culture.[102] Secondly, he believed that although the "numinal" dimension of divine "revelation and its *ker-ygma*" cannot be readily communicated, its second, normative dimension can and ought to be.[103]

There are indications in "The Lonely Man of Faith" that this normative element is "halakhic" in character.[104] If this is the case, there are still further questions that must be asked if an appropriate grasp of Soloveitchik's theological outlook is to be acquired.

When speaking of cultural translation, Soloveitchik did not specify which aspect of culture he had in mind. Is faith to be converted into the categories of contemporary psychology, sociology, or ethics? Or if, as is often the case, into one or another school of philosophy, then which one? Describing the mind-set of the man of culture as he did, the type of philosophy will have to be either "modern" in the strict sense of the word (idealist, rationalist) or "contemporary" (naturalist, pragmatist, or positivist). Whatever the case, the theology that results will be closely akin to the old, apologetic thinking. Soloveitchik did not provide his readers with answers to the above questions. Whether or not he has done so by example of his writings is questionable.

Soloveitchik is a neo-orthodox theologian. His neo-orthodoxy, however, is twofold. Ideologically, he represents the modern Orthodox movement inspired by Samuel Raphael Hirsch. Theologically, he is a representative of the Jewish and Protestant neo-orthodox thought that developed in Germany after the First World War.[105]

The latter is a theology for repentant returners from modernity to pre-modern, traditional modes of thought. This return does not, however, call for the exclusion of modernity. It is not fundamentalist or orthodox in this sense. It seeks, rather, to revive biblical models of thinking together with their traditional interpretations, and to establish a dialectical relationship between the premodern and the modern as a "third way" which points beyond heteronomy and autonomy, fundamentalism and liberalism. In general, the new theology became known as dialectical, existentialist, or neo-orthodox theology. More particularly, it was distinguished as neo-Reformationist, neo-Thomist, neo-Hasidic, neo-Midrashic, and the like. It might be said that Soloveitchik is writing a Jewish theology which is bound neither within the limits of reason (Kant), nor created out of the sources of reason (Cohen), but is, rather, a dialectical mixture of existentialist and idealist, aggadic and halakhic: a neohalakhic theology. In what sense Soloveitchik's writings are "halakhic" is far from easy to determine.

The term "halakhic" might mean at least three things when applied to Soloveitchik's major theological writings: (1) he is writing a theology *of* halakha, (2) he is focusing upon and using theological insights derived from halakha, (3) methodologically, his approach is halakhic.

In "The Man of Halakha," and in a more subtle way, "The Lonely Man of Faith," Soloveitchik utilized philosophical methods to examine and describe the nature and significance of halakhic man: his way of thinking, perceiving, and being in the modern world.[106] Taking the latter as his subject matter, Soloveitchik wrote a theology *of* halakha.

His writings are halakhic, too, in the sense that they employ concepts and categories from the halakha to illustrate and support his theological views.[107] His essays are not exclusively halakhic, however, since as a dialectical thinker, he employs, equally, nonhalakhic materials: classical, medieval, and modern philosophies, Jewish and non-Jewish; as well as considerable aggadic, midrashic, and hasidic materials. This point has not been lost on Soloveitchik's commentators. Rackman, for instance, has written that Soloveitchik is "trying to fuse the emotional intensity of existentialism with the hard logic of rationalism."[108] Hillel Goldberg contended that his theology is an "intermixing of philosophical and Talmudic terminology."[109] For David Singer and Moshe Sokol, Soloveitchik joins "the claims of Litvak intellectualism on the one side and a Hasidic-like affirmation of the emotions on the other."[110] Many commentators were slow in realizing that Soloveitchik's thought was influenced by Hasidisim. As a leading representative of Lithuanian, Talmudic rationalism, and with a doctorate on the thought of Hermann Cohen, it seemed evident that Soloveitchik would show little appreciation for Hasidic thought. Thus, Borowitz wrote in 1968 that Soloveitchik's "The Man of Halakha" is "a *mitnaged,* anti-Hasidic phenomenology of awesome proportions." By 1983, Borowitz came to agree with most commentators that Hasidic thought has played an important role in Soloveitchik's theology.[111]

It would be difficult to defend the assertion that Soloveitchik's theological writings are halakhic in a methodological sense. For Soloveitchik, halakha is "a mode of thinking, a way of interpreting man and his environment" and its "methodological approach demands the highest level of abstraction and conceptualization."[112] Halakhic man, he maintains, is "cognitive man," or "theoretical man."[113] He cannot tolerate obscurity and mystery but seeks to establish a world view which is fixed, logical, and lawful. His methodological outlook is based on the principles of consistency and coherence, system and demonstration. He uses language economically, taking particular care not to waste words. Halakhic man, as Soloveitchik describes him, is a "cognitive man" par excellence. His penchant for system, his idealist and rationalist approach to reality, would require that theology be of the ordinary type: well argued, logically consistent, and definitive.

Soloveitchik's major theological essays, "Halakhic Man" and "The Lonely Man of Faith," are halakhic in that they take as their subject matter the halakha and the "man of halakha," and because they use halakhic categories and terminology. However, these essays are not halakhic in methodology and style. For Soloveitchik, "Halakhic Man" is but a "patchwork of scattered reflections, a haphazard collection of fragmentary observations." The essay, he wrote, "is devoid of scientific precision, of substantive and stylistic clarity. Indeed, it is an indifferent piece of work."[114] In his introduction to "The Lonely Man of Faith," Soloveitchik wrote that what he says therein derives neither "from philosophical dialectics, abstract speculation, or detached impersonal reflections." On the contrary, he maintained: "Instead of talking theology, in the didactic sense, eloquently and in balanced sentences, I would like, hesitantly and haltingly, to confide in you, and to share with you some concerns which weigh heavily on my mind."[115]

If Soloveitchik's essays are understood to be halakhic in content, they are most certainly aggadic, that is, midrashic and homiletic, in style. In his preface to *Halakhic Man,* Lawrence Kaplan maintained that the work is "a unique almost unclassifiable work," written in "an allusive and complex literary style."[116] Similarly, Borowitz wrote that reading Soloveitchik's writings is a unique and demanding experience, for "with Rabbi Soloveitchik as with Heschel, the style is critical to the effect of the thought."[117]

Other commentators have been more specific in characterizing the uniqueness of Soloveitchik's style of writing theology. Arnold Wolfe maintained that Soloveitchik is a "midrashist of inordinate power and skill."[118] Silberman described his style as "typological *midrash.*"[119] Berkovits called it "homiletic,"[120] and Goldberg, "philosophically informed homiletics."[121] Two commentators have contended that Soloveitchik's homiletic-aggadic style is typical of Jewish theology in general. In Goldberg's opinion, "Soloveitchik follows in a time-honored tradition of seminal Jewish thinkers, from Philo to Judah Halevi to the Baal Shem Tov, who favored homiletical or other forms of unystematic expression."[122] David Hartman has written that in Soloveitchik's theological works, there is "a skillful joining together of aggadic and halakhic texts in order to uncover common themes and concepts." Moreover, he attempts to demonstrate "the philosophic relevance of *aggadic midrash,* the narrative-parable form of rabbinic literature often considered to be popular and unworthy of serious analysis."[123]

Although Soloveitchik has shared in many respects a common theological agenda with Herberg, Heschel, and Fackenheim, he differs from them on some important issues. For example, whereas they have attributed theological significance to Jewish history, and championed the cause of theological ecumenicalism, Soloveitchik's approach is, by comparison, ahistorical and anti-ecumenical.

Soloveitchik's ahistorical outlook may be attributed to the threefold influence on his theology of halakhic, midrashic, and existentialist thought.

Fackenheim and Hartman were convinced by the 1967 Arab-Israeli War that the establishment of the Jewish state represented the Jewish people's return into history. In writings published soon thereafter, they faulted the traditional rabbinic attitudes, defined by Fackenheim as "midrashic" and Hartman as "halakhic," for failing to adequately deal with the historical events of the Holocaust and reborn Jewish state.[124] Hartman wrote that "the greatness of halakhic man was his commitment to law which in effect made him immune to history. The tragedy of halakhic man, however, is that Halakha failed to respond adequately when the Jewish people consciously re-entered history."[125] According to Hartman, a major shortcoming of Soloveitchik's halakhic theology is its failure to confront the changing conditions of empirical history.

Another reason for Soloveitchik's ahistoricism may be found in his commitment to classical existentialist philosophy. Existentialism developed in conscious opposition to Hegelian and other schools of historicism that reduced God to an evolving process in history, and defined human redemption in terms of the inevitable progress of reason in history. Religious existentialists have tended to be radically ahistorical, placing great stress on the notion of individual self-redemption by means of immediate faith experiences which transcend reason and history in the here-and-now. Jewish existentialists have therefore often been ahistorical or even antihistorical in outlook. Rosenzweig, for example, regarded the Jewish people as transhistorical, existing outside world history. The early writings of most religious existentialists in America exhibited a similar disregard for Jewish history. However, this situation changed in the 1960s when Herberg, Fackenheim, Hartman, and Heschel began to assign more theological significance to history in their writings. For the most part, Soloveitchik's works have remained ahistorical.[126]

Herberg, Fackenheim, Heschel and a majority of the younger generation of Jewish theologians have addressed themselves to all denominations within the Jewish community and have actively engaged in theological dialogue with non-Jews. Until recently, Soloveitchik has shown little concern for communicating his views outside his own Orthodox community.[127] Thus, for many years his theological views were shared only with a few close friends and disciples. When he did begin to publish his theological essays, they were often written in Hebrew or Yiddish and appeared in Orthodox journals with limited distribution.

Soloveitchik has been one of the few Jewish theologians in America to oppose theological dialogue with Christians. Outlined in the 1964 article "Confrontation," his position was adopted that year by the Orthodox movement's Rabbinical Council of America.[128] Soloveitchik's anti-ecumenicalism is puzzling, for it appears to repudiate his overall religious and theological commitments. For instance, Soloveitchik is a leading representative of modern Orthodoxy, a movement based on the continuing dialogue between traditional Judaism and modern culture and thought. It appears strange, therefore, that he is unwilling to confront Christians in dialogue. This is especially odd, too, since Soloveitchik's theological writings are very much the product of his own confrontation with Western, and especially Christian, thought. In fact, he is often more ready to attribute his philosophical principles to Christian than to Jewish sources, namely, to Kierkegaard, Barth, Heiddeger, Otto, James, Brunner, and Niebuhr. And in such articles as "Confrontation" and "The Lonely Man of Faith," Soloveitchik emphasizes the importance of living in and entering into dialogue with two communities: the individual's faith community and the modern, secular community. The logic of Soloveitchik's thought would seem to support interfaith, theological dialogue. Most of his followers among the younger generation of Orthodox theologians have taken this to be Soloveitchik's true message. Why, then, has Soloveitchik counseled modern Orthodox Jews to refrain from such dialogue? Can his public positions always be taken at face value? According to Emanuel Rackman, they cannot.

In "Soloveitchik: On Differing with My Rebbe," Rackman voiced his frustration at what he considered to be Soloveitchik's frequent failure to assert what he believed to be true in public for fear of the social consequences that might result. Commenting on the fact that many of the younger generation of Orthodox intellectuals have been more outspoken than Soloveitchik in regard to their beliefs and commitments, Rackman wrote that, unlike the Rav, they "are often less timid with regard to the correctness of their views because their sense of security would appear to be greater than his."[129] It would seem, therefore, that whereas Soloveitchik experienced a serious clash between his traditional background and the modern world, the younger generation, born and educated in America or Israel, is far more confident and secure when confronting the non-Jewish world. As a result, in Rackman's opinion, they are doing what Soloveitchik would like to do, but cannot get himself to do.[130]

The writings of Heschel, Fackenheim, and Soloveitchik represent three distinct responses to the "crisis of modernity." This chapter has attempted only to outline their views in respect to the "Question of Jewish Theology," namely, the nature, function, and relevancy of Jewish theology for today.

8. FROM WHENCE WE HAVE COME

In the years immediately following the Second World War (1945–1950), Will Herberg championed the cause of the new Jewish theology on university campuses, at theological seminaries, before rabbinical conventions, and in well-known publications. Because he proclaimed a radically different way of thinking, it was no surprise that he would come into confrontation with representatives of established forms of Jewish thought and practice. A lone figure, he could not at first count on the support of others to help him present his case. Milton Steinberg, who had helped Herberg gain a forum within rabbinic circles, died before their theological partnership could bear fruit. It was not until 1951 that Herberg was able to secure his theological position. With the publication of his *Judaism and Modern Man* and Heschel's *Man Is Not Alone,* the new Jewish theology was "on the map," showing itself to be a viable new force in American intellectual life.

Herberg and Heschel were often depicted as charismatic, prophetic personalities, proclaiming the Word of God to a sinful generation. This reputation derived not only from their understanding of authentic theology and religion as biblical and prophetic, but because they were public figures who brought their theological insights to bear upon the social and political issues of the day.

As they became more involved in the latter, their audience grew beyond the boundaries of the Jewish community to include the nation as a whole. Herberg became a significant influence on Christian thought and eventually obtained a teaching position at Drew University, a Methodist institution. Having moved from the Left to the Right politically, he became the religion editor of William Buckley's *National Review. Judaism and Modern Man,* which Milton Steinberg called "the book of the generation on the Jewish religion," was reissued numerous times during the 1970s and early 1980s.[1] Since Herberg's death in 1977, there has been a major symposium and at least one doctoral dissertation devoted to his life and work, and there have been published two collections of his writings and two biographical studies.[2]

Heschel was, and probably still is, the best known Jewish theologian in the United States. Criticized at first for being an otherworldly mystic, and lacking the rigor and sophistication that some scholars would consider requisite for a rabbi, philosopher, and scholar, he became the mentor of a younger generation of Jewish thinkers and came to be recognized outside the organized Jewish community as an important representative of American Jewry.[3]

Heschel's influence as a theologian has waned little since his death in 1972. His books continue to be published, republished, and translated in the United States and elsewhere, and commentaries on his life and work continue to appear as journal articles, doctoral dissertations, and book-length studies. In observance of his tenth *yahrzeit,* a number of symposia dedicated to his work were held in the United States.[4] Heschel did much to bring respect and honor to the profession of Jewish theology.

Although highly regarded as a philosopher and theologian within academic and rabbinic circles, Fackenheim did not become well known as a theologian until the end of the 1960s. Before that time, he had published important scholarly works in the areas of classical, medieval, and modern philosophy, and a large number of theological essays in journals. The former were available to other scholars in the field, the latter primarily to readers of *Judaism* and *Commentary.* It was not until the appearance in 8 of *Quest for Past and Future* and *God's Presence in History* that he be-to appeal to a wider audience both in the Jewish and non-Jewish communities.

For the first twenty years of his theological career (1947–1967), Fackenheim addressed himself to issues which were of typical concern to the new generation of theologians. In *God's Presence in History* (1969–1970) and *The Jewish Return into History* (1978), he moved from strictly existentialist concerns for the individual and community to recognition of the centrality of Jewish history in general, and of the Holocaust and Jewish state in particular. Adopting a confrontational, "prophetic" stance reminiscent of Herberg and Heschel, Fackenheim increasingly devoted himself in the 1970s to awakening the consciousness of the general public to the theological implications of the Holocaust for the modern world.

Many of Fackenheim's writings during this time were popular rather than academic, yet he did not abandon his role as a professional philosopher and theologian. Two excellent works attest to this: *Encounters between Judaism and Modern Man* (1973) and *To Mend the World* (1982). Fackenheim has helped create a new respect for Jewish theology in America by giving it a combined rigor and passion it had formerly lacked.

In a 1952 *Commentary* article Emanuel Rackman complained that although Soloveitchik had anticipated much of Herberg's general outlook, that fact was little known since the Rav published so little.[5] Today, Soloveitchik's theological outlook is better known. There are many book-length collections of his essays, lectures, and public addresses, as well as a growing body of commentaries on his work. Recently published in English, Soloveitchik's *Halakhic Man* and *The Halakhic Mind* now reach a wide audience in the United States. His major writings have appeared in Hebrew and are published in Israel.[6] Increasingly, classes and lectures devoted to Soloveitchik's theology have been given at educational institutions in the United States and Israel.

It has not been the purpose of this book to determine whether the theological vocation in the United States has been a success, but rather to locate the conditions for its development and to chart the course it has taken since its beginning after the Second World War. It is worthwhile, however, to list some of its achievements and shortcomings, judged according to the degree to which Jewish theologians have realized certain objectives.

If the task of the theologian *qua* theologian is to produce (a) a unified and comprehensive, objective and logically consistent system, and/or (b) a body of literature in which the theologian's statements are clear and consistent, his concepts well-defined, and his subject matter systematically treated, then it must be said that American Jewish theologians have failed in both respects to write theology as it ought to be written. As religious existentialists, they have opposed the writing of theological *systems*. As theologians, they have often paid too little attention to the basic principles of writing theology in a *systematic* way. They have, with few exceptions, produced a body of literature which tends to be fragmentary, subjective, and unsystematic.

American Jewish theologians have often suggested that their brand of theology was capable of overcoming the "crisis of modernity," and could help bring about the spiritual renewal of American and world Jewry and Judaism. If these claims are to be taken seriously, it must be said that so far, American Jewish theologians have failed to realize these objectives.

Although Jewish theology has earned its rightful place within the intellectual community, it still plays a secondary role to that of religious ideology within the rabbinate, the synagogue, and institutionalized Jewish life in general. Jewish theologians have failed to make their discipline the primary mode of Jewish religious thinking in America.[7]

These are some of the failings of American Jewish theologians. What about their achievements?

American theologians have succeeded in making Jewish theology a legitimate and respected enterprise within the Jewish and non-Jewish intellectual communities. Books in Jewish theology have proven to be marketable items in a highly competitive publishing world. They continue to be published, translated, and commented upon forty years after the beginning of American Jewish theology. Courses in American Jewish theology are taught in Christian seminaries and colleges, secular universities, rabbinical schools, synagogues, Sunday schools, and Hillel Foundations.

American Jewish theologians have kept alive the theological revival that began in Germany between the world wars. They successfully transplanted it to American soil and helped create a younger generation of Jewish theologians who now teach Jewish theology at academic institutions in the United States, Israel, and elsewhere.

Jewish theologians not only introduced new trends in religious thinking to American Jews; they have created original theologies which are both American and Jewish.

These theologies are *American*. They were written in America, by American citizens, in the English language and American idiom, for a largely American audience.[8] The continuing popularity of Jewish theology in America attests to the fact that it provides certain segments of the intellectual community with answers to their spiritual and intellectual questions.

American Jewish theology is *Jewish*, not only because it is written by theologians who happen to be Jewish. American Jewish theologians have done much to realize Rosenzweig's objective, namely, to ground all future Jewish theology in traditional rabbinic sources. Mendelssohn, Cohen, Buber, and Rosenzweig were not rabbis. Most Jewish theologians in America combine rabbinic training with doctorates in philosophy and theology from secular universities. They have attempted to ground Jewish theology in Halakha, Midrash, Bible, and Kabbala, and have stressed the primacy of Jewish tradition (Revelation) over modern, secular philosophy (Reason). This has given credence to their claims to be writing theologies that are authentically Jewish.

This book has traced the development of American Jewish theology up to 1980, focusing on a single but dominant school, religious existentialism, and dealing primarily with several of its major representatives: Herberg, Heschel, Soloveitchik, and Fackenheim. What has occurred in Jewish theology since 1980? What might be expected of it in the future?

American Jewish theology has traversed a number of stages. Between 1945 and 1967 Jewish theologians sought to achieve legitimacy for their discipline, and to create a theology that would treat issues facing American Jewry at the time, for example, modernity, secularism, assimilation, self-identity, and renewal. After 1967, Jewish theology entered a stage in which the Holocaust and the Jewish state became central issues. By the 1980s, these two concerns resulted in enhanced Jewish-Christian theological dialogue, and the encounter in Israel of American and Israeli religious thinkers. A third important development has been the establishment of a formal academy for Jewish philosophy devoted to the revitalization of American Jewish philosophy. Yet a fourth has been the beginning of a Jewish feminist theology as part of the larger feminist movement.

(1) The theology that emerged in Europe after the First World War was very much the product of an intellectual exchange among Jewish and Christian theologians. Buber, Rosenzweig, Tillich, Barth, and others shared a common intellectual milieu. They met, corresponded, studied each other's writings, and created, from within their own religious traditions, points of view that were sometimes antithetical, and often strikingly similar.

Heschel, Soloveitchik, and Fackenheim were exposed to this intellectual atmosphere during their student days in Berlin, and discovered one similar to it in America after 1945. Except for Soloveitchik, who opposed interfaith dialogue of a theological nature, Herberg, Steinberg, Heschel, Fackenheim, and a younger generation of American theologians have engaged in all levels of interfaith work.[9] Without apologetics, and speaking a theological language common to Jews and Christians, they have confronted Christian thinkers on issues of vital importance to both faiths.

Today this dialogue is being carried on by a group of dedicated scholars and theologians. On the Jewish side, for example, there are such persons as Eugene Borowitz, Jakob Petuchowski, David Hartman, Judith Plaskow, Irving Greenberg, Susannah Heschel, Michael Wyschogrod, Annette Daum, Stuart Rosenberg, Leon Klenicki, and Emil Fackenheim; on the Christian side, Rosemary Reuther, Gregory Baum, Franklin Littel, Carol Christ, Franklin Sherman, Elaine Pagels, John Pawlikowski, Paul Van Buren, Deborah McCauley, David Tracey, Thomas Idinopulos, Roy and Alice Eckardt, Harry James Cargas, and Eva Fleischner.

The Jewish-Christian agenda is varied. Some thinkers have dealt with topics concerning respective notions of chosenness, covenant, God, revelation, the situation of women, the Holocaust, and the State of Israel. There are theologians who have called for an end to Christian missionary efforts directed toward Jews, and who have repudiated Christian supersessionist doctrines. Many Christian thinkers have called upon their coreligionists to radically rethink their religion's doctrines regarding the Jewish people, its religion, and its homeland, and to recognize that Christian anti-Jewish and anti-Semitic teaching was in large part responsible for the Holocaust.

The Jewish-Christian dialogue is a major achievement of American theologians. It has steadily increased in momentum since 1945, and will probably continue to do so in the foreseeable future.

(2) The revolution in Jewish theology that took place in Germany between the world wars created a generation of religious thinkers, some of whom emigrated to North America, for example, Heschel, Soloveitchik,

and Fackenheim; and others who settled in Israel: Martin Buber, Gershom Scholem, Ernst Simon, Shmuel Bergman, Julius Guttman, and Yeshaiahu Leibowitz. The latter, in turn, helped to produce a new generation of Israeli religious thinkers: Zwi Werblowsky, Nathan Rotenstreich, Pinchas Peli, Rivka Horowitz, Avraham Shapira, Aviezer Ravitzky, Adin Steinsaltz, Eliezer Schweid, Joseph Dan, and Moshe Idel.

Although Israelis have excelled in most areas of religious thought and scholarship, they have not yet produced an Israeli Jewish theology. However, there are indications that this situation will soon change. Some of the conditions that helped give rise to theological activity in American after the Second World War are now present in Israel: a postwar, third-generation sensibility within sectors of the intellectual community; the popularity of existentialist philosophy, theology, and literature; and the influence of "emigré" theologians from North America now living in Israel such as Emil Fackenheim, Eliezer Berkovits, David Hartman, Emanuel Rackman, Shubert Spero, and Paul Mendes-Flohr.

American theologians are now working together with Israeli-educated thinkers, studying, translating, teaching, and writing about contemporary Jewish thought, especially that of Buber, Rosenzweig, Heschel, and Soloveitchik. In addition, they are writing original studies on Jewish ethics, halakha, Zionism, and theology. Perhaps the closest thing at present to an Israeli Jewish theology in the making can be found in the writings of Eliezer Schweid and David Hartman.[10]

Although Hartman and Schweid differ on many issues, they agree on one important point: Both men are convinced that a vital Israeli Jewish theology must learn from, but not imitate, models of Jewish philosophy and theology created in diasporas past and present. Jewish life in a Jewish state is far different from and broader in scope than in America and elsewhere. As Hartman maintains, the Israeli theologian faces the awesome awareness that in Israel Jewish ideas touch the life-and-death issues, affecting the future, not only of his or her children and grandchildren, but of the total social, political, cultural, and religious life of the nation.[11]

It is in the writings of Schweid and Hartman, as well as others in Israel, that we may find the seeds of a future theology which is authentically Jewish and Israeli.

(3) The Academy for Jewish Philosophy was established in 1979 with the purpose of promoting the development of Jewish philosophy and theology. In his introduction to the proceedings of the organization's 1980 meeting, academy chairman Norbert Samuelson wrote that American Jewry has failed to produce a significant body of high-quality philosophical and theological literature.[12] In his opinion, the religious thought of Buber and

Rosenzweig (and by implication, all American Jewish theology that derives from it) is the product of the German-Jewish experience and therefore not applicable to the situation of American Jewry. In an article entitled, "Jewish Philosophy in the 1980s," Steven Katz argued that American Jewish theology is, with the possible exception of Heschel's writings, little more than a series of mediocre footnotes to the dying prewar existentialism of Buber and Rosenzweig.[13] Those members of the Academy who share the opinions of Samuelson and Katz are studying past and present schools of philosophy hoping to create an American Jewish philosophy based on philosophies other than existentialism.

There is a weakness in this critique of American Jewish thought, and a problem with the goal of discovering an alternative to religious existentialism.

In their criticism of American Jewish theology, Samuelson and Katz overlook the fact that after 1945, existentialism became the dominant, but not the only trend in Jewish thought. Important contributions have been made by Jewish thinkers working with other models of philosophy, for example, Milton Steinberg, Simon Greenberg, Robert Gordis, Eliezer Berkovits, Roland Gittelsohn, Alvin Reines, Harold Schulweis, Samuel Cohon, Levi Olan, Jacob Kohn, and Marvin Fox. Furthermore, a number of important books were published during the 1980s which lend support to the view that the postwar revolution in American Jewish theology has not come to an end. Fackenheim's *To Mend the World* and Wyschogrod's *The Body of Faith* are among the most exciting works in Jewish theology to appear in quite some time. In spite of the position he took in the aforementioned essay, Katz praised *To Mend the World*. On the inside of that book, Katz was quoted as saying that "Emil Fackenheim has written the most important work in Jewish philosophy in the last two decades." Similarly, Eisen wrote on the dust jacket of Wyschogrod's book that "this is quite simply, the most stimulating work of Jewish theology to appear in many a year—and one of the most important."[14] Although less philosophically sophisticated, Kushner's *When Bad Things Happen to Good People* showed, by appearing at the top of national bestseller lists, that mainstream Jewish theology still enjoys widespread popularity.[15]

The search by many academy members for a philosophy that can serve the needs of a future American Jewish thought is not without difficulty. This task was easier in previous eras when the *Zeitgeist* was represented by a single school of philosophy. Today, philosophers are confronted with a plethora of competing philosophies, most of which originated, like the existentialism of Buber and Rosenzweig, in Europe prior to the Second World War. This is the case, for instance, with the philosophies of logical positivism, phenomenology, mathematical logic, linguistic analysis, neo-Kantianism, and process philosophy. Pragmatism is perhaps the only authentically American school, and it no longer enjoys the popularity it had in the 1930s.

The Academy has published two collections of essays, originally written for presentation at its annual meetings between 1980 and 1985.[16] The subject matter is varied and the contributors many. Some of the latter are Barry Kogan, Kenneth Seeskin, Steven Schwarzschild, Menachem Kellner, Steven Katz, Jacob Agus, Norbert Samuelson, Arthur Hyman, David Novack, David Bleich, Eugene Borowitz, Seymour Feldman, Alfred Ivry, and Jacob Staum. The quality of these essays is of the highest order—sophisticated, professional, clear, and well argued. Many provide a welcome and timely addition to Jewish existentialism, although there is no evidence to show they have replaced it.

(4) Two highly significant books which have appeared in recent years are Carol Christ and Judith Plaskow's *Womanspirit Rising* and Susannah Heschel's *On Being a Jewish Feminist*. Essays published in these anthologies represent the beginnings of a Jewish feminist theology.[17]

Although Jewish feminists have made major contributions to most fields of Jewish scholarship, they have until recently produced little in the area of Jewish theology. Plaskow, Heschel, and others have done much to amend this situation. In Plaskow's opinion, the Jewish women's movement has failed to recognize the need for Jewish theology because it has addressed itself primarily to external consequences, specific laws and practices. She argues that theological presuppositions are the actual underlying causes of gender discrimination. By neglecting theology Plaskow maintains, the movement has been a civil rights movement rather than one for women's liberation. "It has focused on getting women a piece of the Jewish pie; it has not wanted to bake a new one!"[18]

How, more specifically, can Jewish theology serve the women's movement? According to Susannah Heschel, a Jewish feminist theology ought to locate the causes for the exclusion of women from Jewish thought and practice and develop new interpretations of Judaism that will support feminist values and allow Jewish women full religious expression. "It must apply feminism's concern for women's dignity and humanity in examining the meaning of religious symbols, traditions, and beliefs and strive to give aners to humankind's ultimate questions."[19]

Feminist theologians like Susannah Heschel and Judith Plaskow are heirs to the past thirty-five years of American Jewish theology. Professionally trained theologians, they combine their commitment to the women's movement with academic careers in the fields of Jewish theology and religion.[20]

Methodologically, they define their discipline as Jewish "theology" rather than "philosophy," and work within the general context of religious existentialism and phenomenology. Their agenda is radical, delving to the root-causes of issues; their ultimate goal revolutionary, aiming at the liberation of Jewish women and the transformation and renewal of Judaism. Although still in its formative stages, Jewish feminist theology ought to take its place at the forefront of American Jewish theology in the next decade.

NOTES

1. INTRODUCTION

1. For a discussion of the situation of Jewish theology in relation to the "second" and "third generations," see Arnold Eisen, *The Chosen People in America: A Study in Jewish Religious Ideology* (Bloomington: Indiana University Press, 1983): 7–12, 100–102, 117–118, 127–182. Eisen's study is commendable for its distinction between religious ideology, philosophy, and theology. The "second generation" tended to confuse these distinct modes of thought. For brief discriptions of the situation of Jewish theology in America prior to the Second World War, see the following: Simon Noveck, ed., *Great Jewish Thinkers of the Twentieth Century: B'nai B'rith Great Books Series, I* (Washington, D.C.: B'nai B'rith Department of Adult Jewish Education, 1963): 213–225; Ira Eisenstein, foreword to *Contemporary Jewish Philosophies*, by William Kaufman (New York: Reconstructionist Press and Behrman, 1976): ix-x; Steven Katz, *Jewish Philosophers* (New York: Bloch, 1975): 197–201, 205–207, 244–257.

2. See, for example, Eisen, *Chosen*, passim; P. I. Rose, ed., *The Ghetto and Beyond: Essays on Jewish Life in America* (New York: Random House, 1969): 8, 129; Herbert J. Gans, "The Origin and Growth of a Jewish Community in the Suburbs," in Marshall Sklare, ed., *The Jews: Patterns of an American Group* (New York: Free Press, 1958): 209; Will Herberg, "Religious Trends in American Jewry," in Harold U. Ribalow, ed., *Mid-Century* (New York: Beechurst Press, 1955): 252.

3. See Eisen, *Chosen*, p. 8. An exact definition and dating of these "generations" (or "generation" in general) is notoriously complex and imprecise. For discussions concerning these difficulties see Karl Mannheim, "The Problem of Generations," in his *Essays on the Sociology of Knowledge,* ed. and trans. Paul Kecskemeti (New York: Oxford University Press, 1952): 276–320; Bennett M. Berger, "How Long is a Generation?" *British Journal of Sociology* 11 (1960): 10–23; Alan B. Spitzer, "The Historical Problem of Generations," *American Historical Review* 78 (December 1973): 1353–1385. In this book we will follow Eisen's usage of "second" and "third" generation, while noting two reservations: (1) Not all sociologists would equate, as Eisen does, twenty-five years with a generation; (2) A generation does not "come of age" all at once. Therefore, Eisen's dating of the "second" and "third" generations of American Jews as having been of age between 1930–1955 and 1955–1980, respectively, might better be designated more flexibly as 1925/30–1950/55, and 1950/55–1975/80. By the time Herberg published his 1954–1955 studies of the "third generation," the latter had been around

for some time and had already begun to produce a body of theological literature.

4. Judith R. Kramer and Seymour Leventman, *Children of the Gilded Ghetto: Conflict Resolutions of Three Generations of American Jews* (New Haven: Yale University Press, 1945): 30.

5. Eisen, *Chosen*, p. 9.

6. Ibid., p. 127.

7. See Marcus Lee Hansen, *The Problem of the Third Generation Immigrant* (Illinois: Augustana Historical Society, 1938), and *The Immigrant in American History* (Cambridge: Harvard University Press, 1940). For Will Herberg's application of this study to the situation of American Jewry, see his *Protestant, Catholic, Jew* (New York: Doubleday, 1955).

8. See Irving Kristol, "How Basic Is 'Basic Judaism'?" *Commentary* 5 (January 1948): 27–34, below pp. 36–37; and Emil Fackenheim, *Quest for Past and Future: Essays in Jewish Theology* (Boston: Beacon Press, 1970): 7.

9. See chapter 5.

10. In 1966 Richard Rubenstein wrote: "Regrettably most attempts at formulating a Jewish theology since World War II seem to have been written as if the two decisive events of our time for Jews, the death camps and the birth of Israel, had not taken place" (*After Auschwitz: Radical Theology and Contemporary Judaism* [Indianapolis: Bobbs-Merrill, 1966]: x). Rubenstein was not exaggerating. Of the thirty-eight Jewish thinkers that participated in *Commentary*'s 1966 survey of "The State of Jewish Belief," only Rubenstein stressed the significance of the Holocaust for Jewish life and thought. Heschel and Soloveitchik did not participate in the symposium. Although Fackenheim and Berkovits were participants, they said very little about this issue. See "The State of Jewish Belief: A Symposium," *Commentary* 42 (August 1966): 73–160. It was as a direct result of the 1967 Arab-Israeli War that Berkovits wrote *Faith after the Holocaust* (New York: Ktav, 1973), and A. J. Heschel wrote *Israel: An Echo of Eternity* (New York: Farrar, Straus and Giroux, 1967). Soloveitchik's response to the 1967 war did not produce what at least one of his followers considered an adequate theological position. See David Hartman, *Joy and Responsibility: Israel, Modernity and the Renewal of Judaism* (Jerusalem: Ben-Zvi Posner/Shalom Hartman Institute, 1978): 5–7, 225–229. Fackenheim's views concerning the significance of the Holocaust and reborn Jewish state began to take form in 1967 when he presented a paper at the I. Meier Segals Center for the Study and Advancement of Judaism. This paper was expanded and published in 1970 as *God's Presence in History: Jewish Affirmations and Philosophical Reflections* (New York: New York University Press, 1970).

11. Herberg and Steinberg met regularly between 1947 and 1949 to discuss contemporary Jewish and Christian theology and to plan the establishment of a "Journal of Theological Discussion." See Simon Noveck, *Milton Steinberg: Portrait of a Rabbi* (New York: Ktav, 1978): 216–219, 322,

note 7. These meetings are also discussed in Herberg's letters to Hershel Matt. See, e.g., Will Herberg, Letter to Hershel Matt, 17 October 1949, Will Herberg Archives, Drew University, Madison, New Jersey.

12. See chapter 4.

13. See chapter 3.

14. See chapter 5, note 42.

15. See bibliographies in Nahum Glatzer's *Franz Rosenzweig: His Life and Thought* (New York: Schocken, 1953), and Maurice Friedman's *Martin Buber: The Life of Dialogue* (New York: Harper & Brothers, 1960. Originally published by University of Chicago Press, 1955.)

16. Glatzer, *Rosenzweig;* Friedman, *Buber;* Will Herberg, ed., *The Writing of Martin Buber* (Cleveland and New York: Meridian Books, 1956).

17. Buber was scholar-in-residence at the Jewish Theological Seminary during the 1951–1952 academic year. He delivered the fourth William Alanson White Memorial Lectures at the Washington School of Psychiatry in 1957, and was a guest of Princeton University in 1958.

18. Kaplan's type of religious naturalism was the dominant mode of religious thinking before 1945. See Joseph Zeitlin, *Disciples of the Wise: The Religious and Social Opinion of American Rabbis* (New York: Teachers College of Columbia University, 1945). This was no longer true by the 1960s. See, e.g., Milton Himmelfarb, "The State of Jewish Belief," pp. 71–72, and Arnold J. Wolfe, ed., *Rediscovering Judaism: Reflections of a New Theology* (Chicago: Quadrangle, 1965): 9–11.

19. See chapter 5.

20. See chapters 3 and 4.

21. See chapter 4.

2. THE SITUATION OF AMERICAN JEWISH THEOLOGY IN 1945

1. See for example, Julius Guttman, *Philosophies of Judaism: A History of Jewish Philosophy from Biblical Times to Franz Rosenzweig,* 2nd ed., trans. David W. Silberman, intro. R. J. Zwi Werblowsky (New York: Schocken Books, 1976): 3–19; Isaac Husik, *A History of Medieval Jewish Philosophy* (New York: Atheneum, 1976): xiii–xlix; R. J. Zwi Werblowsky, "A Note on the Relations Between Judaism and Christianity," *Forum for the Problems of Zionism, Jewry, and the State of Israel: Proceedings of the Jerusalem Ideological Conference* 4 (1959): 54–59; and Ephraim Fischoff, "Judaism and Modern Theology," *Central Conference of American Rabbis Yearbook* 66 (1956): 216–230.

2. Arthur Cohen, introduction to *Anatomy of Faith* by Milton Steinberg, ed. Arthur Cohen (New York: Harcourt, Brace & Company, 1960): 55. See also Norman Frimer, "The A-theological Judaism of the American Jewish Community," *Judaism* 11 (Spring 1962): 144–154.

3. Eisenstein, foreword to *Contemporary Jewish Philosophies,* p. ix.

4. Lou Silberman, "Concerning Jewish Theology in North America: Some Notes on a Decade," *American Jewish Yearbook* 70 (1969): 40–41.

5. Arnold Eisen, "Theology, Sociology, Ideology: Jewish Thought in America, 1925–1955," *Modern Judaism* 2 (February 1982): 91.

6. See Samuel S. Cohon, "The Future Task of Jewish Theology," *Reconstructionist* 28 (January 10, 1943): 20.

7. Eugene Borowitz, "The Jewish Need for Theology," *Commentary* 34 (August 1962): 140.

8. Samuel S. Cohon, *Day Book of Service at the Altar as Lived by Samuel S. Cohon, 1888–1959* (Los Angeles: Times Mirror Press, 1978): 125, 130.

9. Himmelfarb, "Jewish Belief," p. 72.

10. Cohon, *Day Book,* p. 130.

11. Will Herberg, Letter to Hershel Matt, 7 December 1947.

12. See Fischoff, "Modern Theology," p. 227.

13. Jakob Petuchowski, "The Question of Jewish Theology," *Judaism* 7 (Winter 1958): 55.

14. See Eli Ginzberg, *Keeper of the Law: Louis Ginzberg* (Philadelphia: Jewish Publication Society, 1966): 145–149.

15. Simon Greenberg, in conversation, 14 August 1982.

16. Louis Finkelstein, in conversation, 19 January 1982.

17. Registrar, Yeshiva University, in conversation, 9 July 1982. A professor of philosophy at the University of Pennsylvania, Husik taught at Yeshiva University in 1928. See Gilbert Klaperman, *The Story of Yeshiva University* (New York: Macmillan, 1969): 149–170; and Aaron Rothkoff, *Bernard Revel: Builder of American Jewish Orthodoxy* (Philadelphia: Jewish Publication Society, 1972): 83.

18. Noveck, *Jewish Thinkers,* p. 213.

19. In the article, "The A-theological Judaism of the American Jewish Community," *Judaism* 11 (Spring 1962), Norman Frimer wrote: " . . . the essence of the behavioral and thought patterns of American Jewry fits most appropriately into the general climate of America as a whole. The very ethos of this land is still a-theological. It is basically activist and pragmatic, with an overtone of distrust for doctrine or ideology. Inwardness and speculation have rarely been advanced as primary American virtues" (p. 145).

See also in this regard, Joseph L. Blau, "What's American about American Jewry?" *Judaism* 7 (Summer 1958): 209–210, and Jacob Agus, *Guideposts in Modern Judaism: An Analysis of Current Trends in Jewish Thought* (New York: Bloch, 1954), passim. It is significant to note that given this "pragmatic" outlook, the only major school of philosophy that is often held to be indigenous to America is the Pragmatism of Peirce, James, and Dewey. Two major schools of religious thought in America in the 1930s and 1940s were influenced by Dewey, namely, the thought of Mordecai Kaplan and Henry Nelson Weiman.

20. Noveck, *Jewish Thinkers,* p. 213.

21. Lou Silberman, "The Theologian's Task," *Central Conference of American Rabbis Yearbook* 73 (1963): 181.

22. Noveck, *Jewish Thinkers,* p. 213.

23. Borowitz, "Need for Theology," p. 140.

24. Silberman, "Theology in North America," p. 40.

25. Cohen, *Anatomy,* p. 155.

26. Samuel S. Cohon, "The Future Task of Jewish Theology," *Reconstructicist* 28 (January 10, 1958): 21.

Before the Second World War, it was difficult for Jews to obtain teaching positions in philosophy or religion departments at American universities. These areas were dominated by Protestant clergymen or laymen with strong Protestant backgrounds. The career of Morris Raphael Cohen is a case in point. See Morris Raphael Cohen, *A Dreamer's Journey: The Autobiography of Morris Raphael Cohen* (New York: Arno Press, 1975) and Leonora Davidson (Cohen) Rosenfield, *Portrait of a Philosopher* (New York: Harcourt, Brace, World, 1962). See, too, in this regard, Solomon Freehof, "Jewish Scholarship in America," in *Jewish Life in America,* ed. Theodore Friedman and Robert Gordis (New York: Horizon Press, 1955): 176.

27. Eisen, "Theology, Sociology, Ideology," p. 99.

28. Robert Gordis, *Commentary* 3 (May 1947): 490.

29. David Novack, "In Memoriam: Professor Samuel Atlas," *Journal of Reform Judaism* 28 (Winter 1981): 92.

30. Before 1945 very few American-educated rabbis possessed advanced degrees in philosophy or theology. Milton Steinberg was one of the few exceptions. He obtained an M. A. in philosophy and earned credits toward a doctorate. See Noveck, *Milton Steinberg,* p. 97; Zeitlin, *Disciples,* pp. 44–45, and Eisen, *Chosen,* pp. 10, 31, 100.

31. Himmelfarb, "Jewish Belief," p. 72.

32. Ephraim Fischoff wrote:

> To how many rabbis, or Jewish intellectuals generally are the theological writers intimately known to whom formal obeisance is made on public occasions—from Geiger through the mid-century figures to Hermann Cohen and beyond? Practically none of the works of these writers is available in English, nor is the situation much better in regard to Mendelssohn and his circle. The accident of linguistic inaccessibility should not be underestimated. For although Kierkegaard died on November 11, 1855, to how many in Anglo-Saxon countries was his massive achievement known before the spate of English translations in the last two decades? Or turning to the Jewish world, to how many of us was the work of Buber, or Rosenzweig, known before English and American translators made them available? ("Modern Theology," p. 219)

Walter Kaufmann held a view similar to that of Fischoff about the role played by the lack of knowledge of the German language and the reception of existentialism and other modes of continental thought in America after the Second World War. See Walter Kaufmann, "The Reception of Existentialism in the United States," *Salmagundi* 3 (Fall/Winter 1969–70): 69–96.

33. Judd Teller, "A Critique of the New Jewish Theology from a Secularist Point of View," *Commentary* 25 (March 1958): 251.

34. See Marshall Sklare, *Conservative Judaism* (New York: Schocken, 1955): 43–65.

35. See, for example, Paul Tillich, *Systematic Theology* I (Chicago: University of Chicago Press, 1951): 71–81.

36. The expression "Orthodox Judaism" is used in this book to refer only to the "modern" variety of orthodoxy usually associated with such institutions as Yeshiva University, the Young Israel movement, the Rabbinical Council of America, and the journal *Tradition*.

37. See James Smart, *The Past, Present and Future of Biblical Theology* (Philadelphia: Westminster Press, 1979): 15.

38. Jakob Petuchowski, "The Question of Jewish Theology," p. 53.

39. Borowitz, "Need for Theology," p. 145.

40. Cohon, *Day Book*, p. 130.

41. Will Herberg rejected the view that the paucity of American Jewish theology was the result of an antitheological bias within traditional Judaism. In "Has Judaism Still Power to Speak? A Religion for an Age of Crisis," *Commentary* 7 (May 1949), Herberg argued:

> If theology is understood in terms more comprehensive than scholastic system-making, Jewish thought has always—at least until recently—been theological. . . . The renunciation of theology in modern times is not so much a continuation of Jewish tradition as a more or less definite break with it, although it must be said that there are aspects of the tradition itself that have made this break possible. This abrupt break with tradition reflects the belated entrance of the Jews into the modern world. For the great mass of Jews in Eastern Europe, there was no Renaissance; within one or two generations, they passed directly from the Middle Ages into modern secularism. For all its great cultural achievements, Emancipation brought confusion and disorientation from which Jewry has not yet recovered. In the rout of traditional Judaism the very notion of religious thinking was all but lost. More, in the self-hatred that this period of demoralization bred, theology was rejected not only because it was theology, but also, and perhaps primarily because it was *Jewish*, because it bore the ghetto-stigma of Jewishness (p. 455).

42. Noveck, *Jewish Thinkers*, p. 214.

43. Eugene Borowitz, "Reform Judaism's Fresh Awareness of Religious Problems: Theological Conference—Cincinnati 1950," *Commentary* 9 (June 1950): 571.

44. Borowitz, "Need for Theology," p. 140.

45. Moshe Davis, *The Emergence of Conservative Judaism* (Philadelphia: Jewish Publication Society, 1963): 284. Related views have been expressed by Hartman, *Joy and Responsibility*, p. 199; Eisen, *Chosen*, p. 11; and David Biale, *Gershom Scholem, Kabbalah and Counter-History* (Boston: Harvard University Press, 1982): 131–132.

46. Davis, *Conservative Judaism*, pp. 283–284.

47. Louis Finkelstein, in conversation, 19 January 1982. The same point of view was expressed by Mordecai Kaplan, in conversation, 5 July 1964.

48. Saul Lieberman, in conversation, 9 June 1981.

49. Will Herberg held this point of view in "Has Judaism Still Power to Speak?" What accounts for the lack of Jewish theology? he asked:

> Is it primarily the desperate insecurity of Jewish existence during the past thirty years that is responsible, as so many have suggested? Has preoccupation with mere survival absorbed so much of Jewish energy as to leave little or none for reflective thought transcending the moment? Insecurity and disaster are nothing new in the history of Israel, but never in the past did they paralyze the sources of spiritual creativity. On the contrary, every great achievement in Jewish religious thought came into being in response to crisis (p. 455).

50. At the very same time that Jewish theology was being neglected, other fields of theoretical work were thriving, for example, studies in the fields of Talmud (Saul Lieberman), Midrash (Max Kadushin and Louis Ginzberg), and History (Louis Finkelstein, Salo Baron, Alexander Marx, and Jacob Rader Marcus).

51. See Abraham Karp, "Toward a Theology for Conservative Judaism," *Conservative Judaism* 10 (Summer 1956): 14–21. Criticizing the lack of philosophical activity in the Conservative movement, Karp declared that rabbis and laymen have turned this "embarrassment into a virtue," and have abandoned their liberal perspective by becoming "ultra traditionalist in pleading that theology has not been the particular *métier* of our people. Ours is a way of life, not a creed or a confessional, runs the argument" (p. 14). See Mordecai Kaplan's reply to Karp, "If Theology Were Our Only Métier," *Conservative Judaism* 11 (Winter 1957): 20–25.

52. These four theologians were of the same generation, biologically and intellectually. Buber was born in 1878, Rosenzweig, Barth, and Tillich in 1886. They studied for a time at the University of Berlin, and shared a similar education in nineteenth-century German philosophy and theology. They experienced the First World War in similar fashion. For them it was a traumatic, conversionary experience which convinced them that nineteenth-century schools of liberalism, rationalism, and idealism were bank-

rupt and in need of being superseded by new modes of language and thought.

3.   THE CALL FOR THEOLOGY

1. See Seymour Siegel, "A Tribute to Will Herberg: A Biographical Sketch," *National Review* 29 (August 5, 1977): 880; and "Will Herberg: A Baal Teshuvah Who Became a Theologian, Sociologist, Teacher," *American Jewish Yearbook* 78 (1978): 529.

2. Will Herberg, "Reinhold Niebuhr: Christian Apologist to the Secular World," *Union Seminary Quarterly* 11 (October 1956): 12.

3. Bob E. Patterson, *Reinhold Niebuhr* (Texas: Word, Inc., 1977): 32–33.

4. See Sidney Hook, "The New Failure of Nerve," (pp. 2–23) and John Dewey's "Anti-Naturalism in Extremis," (pp. 24–39) in *The Partisan Review* 10 (January-February, 1943); Horace Kallen, *Secularism Is the Will of God: An Essay in the Social Philosophy of Democracy and Religion* (New York: Twayne Publishing, 1954); and Henry Nelson Weiman, ed., *Religious Liberals Reply* (Boston: Beacon Press, 1947).

5. See Siegel, "A Tribute to Will Herberg," p. 881, and "Will Herberg: Baal Teshuvah," p. 532. Some of the rabbinical students who aided Herberg in his study of rabbinic sources and Hebrew (which he never adequately learned), later became important representatives of the Conservative movement: Gerson Cohen, Hershel Matt, Monford Harris, and Seymour Siegel.

6. Siegel, "Will Herberg: Baal Teshuvah," p. 532.

7. Will Herberg, "From Marxism to Judaism." *Commentary* 3 (January, 1947): 25–32.

8. Steinberg summed up the appeal Herberg held for many Jewish intellectuals at the time, when in his review of Heberg's "From Marxism to Judaism," he wrote that this essay,

> . . . indicates that Judaism has not lost the power to win souls from among free and uncommited men. And it gives further evidence in support of certain old propositions whose very antiquity conceals their never failing pertinence: the truth that social idealism requires a religious faith on which it may stand, by which its purity shall be preserved and the further truth that of all the world's religious faiths none is better suited to these purposes than Judaism (*The Park Avenue Synagogue Bulletin* 1 [February 17, 1947]: 2).

For a description of the friendship that developed between Steinberg and Herberg, see Noveck, *Milton Steinberg*, pp. 217–222.

9. See, for example, Milton Steinberg, "The Test of Time," in *A Be-*

lieving Jew: The Selected Writings of Milton Steinberg, ed. Maurice Samuel (New York: Harcourt, Brace & Company, 1951): 174–176; "The Theological Issues of the Hour," *Proceedings of the Rabbinical Assembly of America* 13 (1949): 379–380; Noveck, *Milton Steinberg,* pp. 258–260; and "New Currents in Religious Thought," in *Anatomy of Faith,* pp. 246–253.

10. Lou Silberman, review of *Anatomy of Faith* by Milton Steinberg, *Judaism* 10 (Winter 1961): 86.

11. See, for example, Steinberg, *Believing Jew,* pp. 166–178; *Anatomy of Faith,* pp. 246–249.

12. Kristol, "Basic Judaism," p. 28. Kristol, like others of his generation, broke with religious liberalism as the direct result of the Second World War. It was during the First World War that Rosenzweig and Tillich in the German army, Buber, Barth, and Niebuhr on the home front, proclaimed the demise of religious and political liberalism, and set out to replace it with "the new thinking."

13. Ibid., p. 32.

14. In "Crisis Theology and the Jewish Community," *Commentary* 32 (July 1961): 36, Eugene Borowitz wrote:

> Contemporary Jewish thinkers, of whom Steinberg was the most articulate, lacked the courage or the vision to see the problem, much less to provide the answers. Books, journals, and sermons seemed quite satisfied with the liberal formulas and melioristic illusions of the '30s. To read or hear them was to experience the eerie feeling that their authors had been suspended in time or that in their limited vision they had remained oblivious to what meanwhile had happened to mankind. Thus, for men like Irving Kristol, who were preoccupied with the ordeal of Western culture, a Judaism without an emphasis on the problem of sin was "still catastrophically narrow," and was characterized by "intellectual timidity, cultural immaturity." So went the appraisal and the challenge.

15. Silberman, *Anatomy of Faith,* p. 89. See Richard Rubenstein's *Power Struggle* (New York: Charles Scribners Sons, 1974) for a description of his student days at Hebrew Union College and the Jewish Theological Seminary at the time when the views of Buber and Rosenzweig were first being introduced to the American Jewish community.

16. Noveck, *Milton Steinberg,* pp. 222–223.

17. Will Herberg, "Theological Problems of the Hour," *Proceedings of the Rabbinical Assembly of America* 13 (1949): 409–410. Some of Herberg's critics seriously doubted that Judaism had the capacity to answer the questions posed by the postwar crisis. See, for example, Harold Rosenberg, "Pledged to the Marvelous: An Open Letter to Will Herberg," *Commentary* 3 (February 1947): 145–151.

18. Herberg, "Theological Problems," p. 411.

19. Steinberg, "Theological Issues," pp. 208–209.

20. Eugene Kohn, "Theological Problems of the Hour," pp. 429–438. In the proceedings of the conference, Kohn's paper is joined with that of Herberg's paper under the common title: "Theological Problems of the Hour."

21. These impressions were expressed in conversations with Hershel Matt, 4 May 1981, and Seymour Siegel, 1 December 1982.

22. Abraham Joshua Heschel, "The Spirit of Prayer," *Proceedings of the Rabbinical Assembly of America* 17 (1953): 151–178. Other participants in the symposium were Eugene Kohn ("Prayer for the Modern Jew," pp. 179–192), and Arnold Lasker ("Personal Prayer," pp. 231–239). Although not advertised as a "theological discussion," Heschel did his best to make it one.

23. Heschel was not trained as a Conservative rabbi in the United States. Ordained as a young man within the Hassidic community and later at the *Hochschule für die Wissenschaft des Judentums* in Berlin, he was invited to join the staff of Hebrew Union College in 1940, and the Jewish Theological Seminary in 1945.

24. At the time of the 1953 convention, Heschel had already established himself as an important theologian. His publications in English included: *The Quest for Certainty in Saadia's Philosophy* (New York: Feldheim, 1944); *The Earth is the Lord's: The Inner Life of the Jews in Eastern Europe* (New York: Schocken, 1950); *Man Is Not Alone: A Philosophy of Religion* (New York: Farrar, Straus and Young, 1951); and *The Sabbath: Its Meaning for Modern Man* (New York: Farrar, Straus and Young, 1951).

25. Heschel, "Prayer," p. 159.

26. The data represented in Zeitlin's *Disciples of the Wise* was gathered in 1937, and was in some ways outdated by the time the study appeared in print in 1945.

27. Heschel's remarks are quoted by Fritz Rothschild in the latter's article, "Conservative Judaism Faces the Need for Change: In What Direction, How Much, and How?" *Commentary* 16 (November 1953): 448.

28. In addressing the convention, Heschel purposely adopted a confrontational stance. In doing so, he was very much in accord with the theological positions of Buber, Barth, Niebuhr, Tillich, Soloveitchik, Fackenheim, and Herberg. Paul Tillich clearly illustrated this "prophetic" stance when he wrote: "The first word, therefore, to be spoken by religion to the people of our time must be a word spoken against religion. It is the word of the old Jewish prophets spoken against the priestly and royal and pseudo-prophetic guardians of their national religion" *The Protestant Era* (Chicago: University of Chicago Press, 1948): 185–6.

29. See Kohn, "Prayer," pp. 179–191.

30. Rothschild, "Conservative Judaism," pp. 449, 455.

31. A. J. Heschel, "Toward an Understanding of Halacha," *The Central Conference of American Rabbis Yearbook* 63 (1953): 386–409.

32. Albert Plotkin, "Abraham Joshua Heschel: A Tribute," *Central Conference of American Rabbis Journal* 20 (Summer 1973): 78–79.

33. See, for example, Fackenheim's articles "Can We Believe in Judaism Religiously," *Commentary* 6 (December 1948): 521–527; review of "Judaism: A Way of Life" by Samuel S. Cohon, *Commentary* 3 (September 1949): 302–304; and "The Modern Jew's Path to God: Initiating the Great Encounter," *Commentary* 9 (May 1950): 450–457.

34. Fackenheim, *Quest*, p. 7.

35. Ibid.

36. Fackenheim, "Path to God," p. 453.

37. Fackenheim, *Quest*, p. 5.

38. Ibid.

39. For a report of this conference see Eugene Borowitz, "Theological Conference," pp. 567–572.

40. See a progress report on the success of the Institute for Reform Jewish Theology in Bernard Heller, "Report of the Commission on Jewish Theology," *Central Conference of American Rabbis Yearbook* 66 (1956): 68–70.

41. Known as "the Oconomowok Group," some of these theologians presented at the convention a number of important papers, all of which were coordinated in advance to make the greatest impact on their audience. For a discussion of this group and its effect on the Reform movement, see Ben Hamon "The Reform Rabbis Debate Theology: A Report on the 1963 Meeting of the CCAR," *Judaism* 12 (Fall 1963): 479–486, and Gunther Plaut, *The Growth of Reform Judaism: American and European Sources until 1948* (New York: World Union for Progressive Judaism, 1965): 353–355. For a list of papers presented by this group at the conference, see below, note 49.

42. Ben Hamon, "Reform Rabbis," p. 480. "Ben Hamon" is a pseudonym used by a rabbi who was present at the conference.

43. Ibid., p. 486.

44. Part of the reason for this may be that there was no great difference in age between Fackenheim and his colleagues. And, too, Fackenheim lacked the charisma of Heschel and Herberg.

45. This fact was confirmed in conversations with two of Herberg and Heschel's followers, namely, Hershel Matt, 13 December 1982, and Seymour Siegel, 2 March 1981.

46. Although Heschel's disciple Fritz Rothschild has published some good papers in theology, his reputation as a theologian rests primarily upon his commentaries on Heschel's life and work. See, for example, *Between God and Man: An Interpretation of Judaism from the Writings of Abraham J. Heschel*, ed. and intro. Fritz Rothschild (New York: Free Press-Macmillan, 1965). This appears to be the case, as well, with Hershel Matt. Matt has admitted that Herberg often warned him of the dire consequences for his own (Matt's) creative work that such discipleship would present. Hershel Matt, personal conversation, 4 May 1981.

47. The younger generation of Reform theologians was regarded by many to have created a revolution within their movement by replacing the prevailing liberal, idealist orientation with one which was existentialist and neo-orthodox. See Shubert Spero, "Stirrings in Reform Theology," *The Jewish Observer* 1 (May 1964): 13–15; Plaut, *Reform Judaism,* pp. 353–355; and Ben Hamon, "Reform Rabbis," pp. 479–486.

48. According to Marshall Sklare, this is due to the Jewish Theological Seminary's view of education, which, in his opinion, makes it emotionally difficult for students "to act independently of their mentors." See Sklare's *Conservative Judaism* (New York: Schocken, 1955): 212–245. Although there is some truth in Sklare's thesis, it does not account for the independence of two well-known theologians, both of whom studied for a time at the Jewish Theological Seminary: Arthur Cohen and Richard Rubenstein.

49. At the 1952 meeting, for instance, six papers were given at a symposium entitled "Judaism and Existentialism." In 1953 a symposium was held on the subject of "Contemporary Trends in Jewish Theology." At the 1956 gathering there was a symposium on "Judaism and Modern Theology," and Bernhard Heller, chairman of the Reform Institute for Theology, reported to the convention on the progress of the institute's work. In 1963 a number of important papers were delivered by members of the so-called "Oconomowok Group": Lou Silberman's "The Theologian's Task," Samuel Karff's "The Agada as a Source of Contemporary Jewish Theology," Steven Schwarzschild's "The Role and Limits of Reason in Contemporary Jewish Theology," and Eugene Borowitz's "Faith and Method in Modern Jewish Theology." The latter essays are to be found in the *Central Conference of American Rabbis Yearbook* 73 (1963): 173–228.

50. David Wolf Silverman, "Current Theological Trends: A Survey and Analysis," *Proceedings of the Rabbinical Assembly of America* 23 (1959): 71–100. Silverman's study of current trends in theology was devoted almost solely to Protestant theology. Trude Weiss-Rosmarin criticized this fact in "Jewish Theology," *Jewish Spectator* 25 (November 1960): 5–7.

51. Orthodox and Reform theologians and scholars have often ridiculed the Conservative movement for its lack of significant theological activity. See, for example, Bernard Martin, "Conservative Judaism and Reconstructionism in the Last Three Decades," *Journal of Reform Judaism* 25 (Spring 1978): 95–152; Charles Leibman, "The Training of American Rabbis," *American Jewish Yearbook* 69 (1968): 84; Shubert Spero, "Stirring within Reform," p. 15. Some Conservative thinkers have also criticized their movement for its failure to stress the significance of Jewish theology: Arthur Cohen, "The Seminary and the Modern Rabbi," *Conservative Judaism* 13 (Spring 1959): 1–12; Abraham Karp, "Toward a Theology," pp. 14–22.

52. E.g., "Ish Ha-Halakhah," *Talpiot* I (1944): 651–735; and "The Sacred and Profane: Kodesh and Chol in World Perspective," *Hazedek* (May–June, 1945): 4–20.

53. See Emanuel Rackman, "Orthodox Judaism Moves with the Times," *Commentary* 13 (June 1952): 546, 548.

54. Joseph Epstein, introduction to *Shiurei Harav: A Conspectus of the Public Lectures of Rabbi Joseph B. Soloveitchik,* ed. Joseph Epstein, (New York: Hamevaser, Yeshiva University, 1974): 3.

55. Rackman, "Orthodox Judaism," p. 546. See, in this regard, Walter Wurzburger, "The State of Orthodoxy: A Symposium," *Tradition* 20 (Spring 1982): 3–5.

56. Agus, *Guideposts,* pp. 20–51; Eugene Borowitz, "The Typological Theology of Rabbi Joseph B. Soloveitchik," *Judaism* 15 (Spring 1966): 203–210.

57. Rackman, "Orthodox Judaism," p. 546. Rackman noted that the Reform movement was dominated for a time by the "psychological approach" of Joshua Loth Liebman, and the Conservative movement by the "sociological school" of Mordecai Kaplan. Within American Orthodoxy, Leo Jung represented the former approach and Maurice Farbridge the latter. According to Rackman, the "metaphysical" school of Herberg, Heschel, and Fackenheim was represented within American Orthodoxy by Rabbi Soloveitchik.

58. Most of Soloveitchik's published articles originated as public addresses given to Orthodox audiences, and were published by Rabbinical Council of America and Yeshiva University publications such as *Hazedek, Talpiot, Hadarom, Hamevasar, Gesher,* and *Tradition.*

4. A DECADE OF CONTROVERSY

1. See Eugene Borowitz, "The Career of Jewish Existentialism," *Jewish Book Annual* 32 (1974–1975): 44–49; David Sidorsky, "Judaism and the Revolution of Modernity," *The Future of the Jewish Community in America,* ed. David Sidorsky (Philadelphia: Jewish Publication Society, 1973): 3–21; Harold Weisberg, "Ideologies of American Jews," in Oscar J. Janowsky, ed. *The American Jew: A Reappraisal, 1964* (Philadelphia: Jewish Publication Society, 1965): 339–359; Plaut, *Reform Judaism,* pp. 355–363; Eisen, "Theology, Sociology, Ideology," pp. 91, 105.

2. See Kaufmann, "Reception of Existentialism," p. 79.

3. See William Barrett, *Irrational Man: A Study in Existential Philosphy* (New York: Doubleday Anchor, 1958): 3–22.

4. Ibid., pp. 8–9.

5. See, for example, Emil Fackenheim, "In Praise of Abraham, Our Father," *Commentary* 5 (December 1948): 521–527; Joseph Gumbiner, "Existentialism and Father Abraham: A Colloquy with Kierkegaard," *Commentary* 5 (February 1948): 143–148; Milton Steinberg, "Kierkegaard and Judaism," *Menorah Journal* 37 (Spring 1949): 163–180; Marvin Fox, "Kier-

kegaard and Rabbinic Judaism," *Judaism* 2 (April 1953): 160–169; Joseph Narot, "Recent Jewish Existentialist Writing," *Central Conference of American Rabbis Yearbook* 62 (1953): 435–444; Jacob Halevi, "Kierkegaard and the Midrash," *Judaism* 4 (Winter 1955): 13–28. The influence of Kierkegaard on Soloveitchik can be clearly seen in the latter's essays, "Confrontation," *Tradition* 6 (Spring/Summer 1964): 5–30 and "The Lonely Man of Faith," *Tradition* 7 (Summer 1965): 5–67. Heschel's *A Passion for Truth* (New York: Farrar, Straus and Giroux, 1973) was devoted to a comparison of Kierkegaard's life and thought with that of the Baal Shem Tov and the Kotzker Rabbi.

6. See chapter 3, note 4.

7. See chapter 1.

8. Mordecai Kaplan, *Judaism without Supernaturalism* (New York: Reconstructionist Press, 1958): 10–11.

9. Abba Hillel Silver, *Where Judaism Differed* (New York: Collier-Macmillan, 1956): 208.

10. Eugene Borowitz, "Existentialism's Meaning for Judaism," *Commentary* 29 (November 1959): 414; Silberman, "Theology in North America," pp. 40–41.

11. Himmelfarb, "Jewish Belief," p. 72.

12. Eugene Kohn, "The Menace of Existentialist Religion," *Reconstructionist* 17 (January 11, 1952): 14.

13. Ibid., p. 7.

14. Robert Gordis, *Faith for Moderns* (New York: Bloch, 1960): 5.

15. Samuel S. Cohon, "The Existentialist Trend in Theology," *Central Conference of American Rabbis Yearbook* 62 (1953): 372. Cohon's presentation before the assembled rabbis at the conference was similar in purpose to Steinberg's 1949 address to the Rabbinical Assembly of America. Both men sought to educate the American rabbinate in the newest trends in theology.

16. Ibid., p. 385.

17. Milton Steinberg, *As a Driven Leaf* (New York: Behrman House, 1939).

18. See Simon Noveck, "Milton Steinberg's Philosophy of Religion," *Judaism* 26 (Winter 1977): 35–45.

19. Steinberg, "Kierkegaard and Judaism," p. 180.

20. Albert Goldstein, letter, "Correspondence: For and Against Herberg," *Jewish Frontier* 17 (November 1950): 29.

21. Harold Weisberg, "Escape from Reason: A Reply to Will Herberg," *Reconstructionist* 16 (December 1, 1950): 24.

22. See Emil Fackenheim, "Rationalistic Reactions to the 'New Jewish Theology'," *Central Conference of American Rabbis Journal* 26 (June 1959): 42–48. For an account of Mordecai Kaplan's almost "incoherent harangue" at hearing Herberg express his theological views in a symposium held at

the Jewish Theological Seminary, see Herberg, letter to Hershel Matt, 7 July 1950.

23. Fackenheim, "Reactions," p. 45.

24. Jakob Kohn, "The Assault on Reason," *Reconstructionist* 23 (January 24, 1958): 7–12, "Menace," pp. 7–8. Herberg was also called "arrogant," "nihilistic," "pessimistic," and "authoritarian." See, for example, Samuel Sandmel, letter, "Correspondence: For and Against Herberg," p. 28, and Joseph Narot, "Two Authoritarian Critics of Psychoanalysis," *Reconstructionist* 18 (May 16, 1952): 7–13.

25. Weisberg, "Escape," p. 24. In spite of its sensationalistic title, Weisberg's article was one of the few penetrating criticisms of Herberg's thought written at the time.

26. Goldstein, "Correspondence," pp. 28–29.

27. Teller, "New Jewish Theology," p. 252.

28. Goldstein, "Correspondence," p. 28.

29. Robert Gordis, "The Genesis of *Judaism:* A Chapter in Jewish Cultural History," *Judaism* 30 (Fall 1981): 393. It is because of this "horror" over the un-Jewish character of Herberg's picture of Judaism, that Grayzel asked Steinberg to work with Herberg on the manuscript. See Noveck, *Milton Steinberg,* pp. 218, 322, and Herberg's Letter to Hershel Matt, 2 November 1949.

30. See, for example, Rackman, "Modern Orthodoxy," pp. 546–548; Nahum Glatzer, review of *Judaism and Modern Man* by Will Herberg, *Commentary* 13 (March 19): 296–298; Milton Konvitz, review of *Judaism and Modern Man* by Will Herberg, *Saturday Review of Literature* (March 8, 1952): 57–58; Ludwig Lewisohn, review of *Judaism and Modern Man* by Will Herberg, *Congress Weekly* 18 (October 8, 1951): 13–14. In letters to Hershel Matt, Herberg mentions having received letters of high praise from Max Brod, Judah Magnes, David De Sola Pool, and others.

31. Siegel, "Will Herberg: Baal Teshuvah," p. 532.

32. Arthur Cohen, ed., *Arguments and Doctrines: A Reader of Jewish Thinking in the Aftermath* (New York: Harper & Row, 1970): 98.

33. By the middle of the 1950s the expression "the New Jewish Theology," became a convenient designation in the journals "for the type of thought represented by Buber, Rosenzweig, Heschel, and Herberg, among others" (Fackenheim, "Reactions," p. 42). "There were, to be sure, important and capable scholars in the field in the pre-war period. But their audience cannot be compared with those of Heschel, Herberg and others, whose names are to be reckoned with in the Jewish community and in the Christian community" (Seymour Siegel, "Theology, Torah, and the Man of Today," *Conservative Judaism* 16 [Winter/Spring 1962]: 56). See, for example, Teller, "New Jewish Theology," pp. 243–252, and Weiss-Rosmarin, "Jewish Theology" pp. 5–7.

34. Weiss-Rosmarin, "Jewish Theology," pp. 6–7.

35. Meir Ben-Horin, "Via Mystica," *Jewish Quarterly Review* 45 (January 1955): 258. See, too, Ben-Horin's "The Ineffable: Critical Notes on Neo-Mysticism," *Jewish Quarterly Review* 46 (April 1956): 321–354, and "The Ultimate and the Mystery: A Critique of Some Neo-mystical Tenets," *Jewish Quarterly Review* 51 (July 1960): 55–71; (October 1960): 141–156.

36. See, for example, Fackenheim's reviews of Herberg's *Judaism and Modern Man*, in *Judaism* 1 (April 1952): 172–176; and of Heschel's *Man is Not Alone*, in *Judaism* 1 (January 1952): 85–89 and *God in Search of Man*, in *Conservative Judaism* 15 (Fall 1960): 50–53.

37. Fackenheim, "Reactions," pp. 42–45.

38. Emil Fackenheim, "Liberalism and Reform Judaism," *Central Conference of American Rabbis Journal* 21 (April 1958): 4.

39. Weiss-Rosmarin and Ben-Horin were not alone in considering Heschel to be a mystic and poet rather than a serious philosopher or theologian. This was, and perhaps still is, a widespread point of view. Herbert Schneider and Fritz Rothschild have tried to demonstrate that underlying the poetic exterior of Heschel's thought, there is to be found a great deal of philosophical argument, sophistication, and system. See Schneider's "On Reading Heschel's *God in Search of Man:* A Review Article," *Review of Religion* 21 (November 1956): 31–38. Rothschild tried to systematically organize and present Heschel's thought in *Between God and Man*.

40. In his series of articles on "Neo-mysticism," Ben-Horin ridiculed Heschel for his alleged "philagnosy" (love of unenlightenment) and "phobosophy" (the fear of knowledge). See Rothschild's reference to this in the bibliography, *Between God and Man*, p. 292. In contrast to the "second generation" which tended to ridicule Heschel for his "obscurantism" and "mysticism," the "third generation" of religious thinkers were critical yet sympathetic in their approach to Heschel's writings. They did their best to give him a fair hearing. See, for example, Jakob Petuchowski, "Faith as the Leap of Action: The Theology of Abraham Joshua Heschel," *Commentary* 25 (May 1958): 390–397; Maurice Friedman, "Abraham Joshua Heschel: Toward a Philosophy of Judaism," *Conservative Judaism* 10 (Winter 1956): 1–10; Lou Silberman, "The Philosophy of Abraham Joshua Heschel," *Jewish Heritage* 2 (Spring 1955): 23–26; Edmond La B. Cherbonnier, "A. J. Heschel and the Philosophy of the Bible: Mystic or Rationalist?" *Commentary* 27 (January 1959): 23–29; Marvin Fox, "Heschel, Intuition, and the Halakhah," *Tradition* 3 (Fall 1960): 5–15.

41. See, for example, Reinhold Niebuhr, review of *Man is Not Alone* by A. J. Heschel, in *New York Herald Tribune Book Reveiws* (April 1, 1951).

42. Milton Steinberg, "The Outlook of Reinhold Niebuhr: A Description and Appraisal," *Reconstructionist* 11 (December 14, 1945): 10–15. Niebuhr received an honorary doctorate from the Hebrew University of Jerusalem in 1967. Niebuhr's Zionism is discussed in Ronald Stone's "The Zionism of

Paul Tillich and Reinhold Niebuhr," *Jewish Digest* (March-April 1983): 8–16.

43. Steinberg, "New Currents in Religious Thought," *Anatomy of Faith*, p. 294.

44. Steinberg's dialectical approach derived from the bipolar view of logic and reality taught by Morris Raphael Cohen. Cohen was Steinberg's teacher at the City College of New York. See Noveck, *Milton Steinberg*, pp. 18–36.

45. Steinberg, "New Currents," p. 295.

46. Steinberg, "Theological Issues," p. 386.

47. Heschel's essay was entitled "A Hebrew Evaluation of Reinhold Niebuhr." The essay appeared in the book *Reinhold Niebuhr*, ed. Charles W. Kegeley and Robert W. Bretall (New York: Macmillan, 1956). Heschel's article was republished as "A Confusion of Good and Evil," and appears in his *The Insecurity of Freedom: Essays on Human Existence* (New York: Schocken, 1975): 127–149. Heschel delivered the eulogy at Niebuhr's funeral. The latter was published as "Reinhold Niebuhr: A Last Farewell," *Conservative Judaism* 25 (Summer 1971): 62–63.

48. Heschel, "A Confusion of Good and Evil," p. 36.

49. Ibid., p. 133.

50. Ibid., pp. 127–128.

51. Levi Olan, "Reinhold Niebuhr and the Hebraic Spirit: A Critical Inquiry," *Judaism* 5 (Spring 1956): 108–122; Emil Fackenheim, "Judaism, Christianity, and Reinhold Niebuhr: A Reply to Levi Olan," *Judaism* 5 (Fall 1956): 316–324.

52. Olan, "Niebuhr," p. 114.

53. Ibid., p. 122.

54. Fackenheim, "Niebuhr," p. 317.

55. Ibid.

56. For full citation see chapter 3, note 50.

57. Weiss-Rosmarin studied for her doctorate in philosophy (with a dissertation on Hermann Cohen) at the University of Berlin along with Soloveitchik and Heschel. Her dissertation was published as *Religion of Reason: Hermann Cohen's System of Religious Philosphy* (New York: Bloch, 1936).

58. Weiss-Rosmarin, "Jewish Theology," p. 7.

59. Ibid.

60. Petuchowski, "Jewish Theology," p. 24.

61. Ibid. Petuchowski alludes here to his own use of Rosenzweig's ideas in his book, *Ever since Sinai: A Modern View of Torah* (New York: Scribe Publications, 1961).

62. Ibid.

63. Ibid.

64. See Will Herberg, review of *A Believing Jew: The Selected Writings of Milton Steinberg*, ed. Maurice Samuel, in *Commentary* 12 (November 1951):

498. According to Matt, Herberg was convinced that the omission of Steinberg's later writings from *A Believing Jew,* represented an attempt to censure Steinberg's criticisms of liberal Judaism (Hershel Matt, in conversation, 4 May 1981.)

65. For full citation see chapter 2, note 2.

66. Robert Gordis, review of *Anatomy of Faith,* by Milton Steinberg, in *New York Times Sunday Book Review* 10 April 1960.

67. Ira Eisenstein, "An Analysis of Milton Steinberg's *Anatomy of Faith,*" *Conservative Judaism* 14 (Summer 1960): 9. In the same symposium, Jacob Agus criticized Steinberg for having retained his liberal-rationalist outlook which followed "the tradition of German-Jewish scholarship at the Jewish Theological Seminary." This point of view, Agus suggested, defined Judaism exclusively in terms of what is "rational," ignoring the mystical-Hasidic aspects of the Jewish heritage (Agus, "Analysis," p. 3). In "Jewish Theology," Weiss-Rosmarin criticized Steinberg for having encouraged the younger generation of theologians to adopt Christian and existentialist models for writing theology (Weiss-Rosmarin, "Jewish Theology," p. 6).

68. Arthur Zuckerman, "More on *Anatomy of Faith,*" *Reconstructionist* 26 (January 27, 1961): 24–26.

69. Arthur Cohen, "Correspondence: On Steinberg's *Anatomy of Faith,*" *Reconstructionist* 27 (February 24, 1961): 29.

70. Arthur Cohen, "An Analysis of Milton Steinberg's *Anatomy of Faith: A Reply to the Critics,*" *Conservative Judaism* 14 (Summer 1960): 16.

71. Ibid., p. 18.

72. Noveck, *Milton Steinberg,* p. 256.

73. Ibid., p. 249.

74. Ibid., pp. 216–225, 249–267.

5. THE REVIVAL OF THEOLOGY

1. Weisberg, "Escape," p. 17. See also Will Herberg, review of *God in Search of Man,* by A. J. Heschel, in *Christian Century* 73 (April 18, 1956): 486; Heller, "Report," p. 69.

2. Silverman, "Theological Trends," p. 78.

3. Weisberg, "Ideologies," pp. 340, 343.

4. Silverman, Ibid., p. 78.

5. Gordis, *Faith for Moderns,* p. 5.

6. Examples of such thinkers are Herbert Marcuse, C. Wright Mills, Marcus Hansen, Paul Tillich, Reinhold Niebuhr, Will Herberg, Emil Fackenheim, A. J. Heschel, Peter Berger, Robert Bellah, Harvey Cox, Sam Keen, Gordon Kaufman, and Langdon Gilkey.

7. Ludwig Lewisohn claimed that his book, *The Permanent Horizon* (New

York and London: Harper & Brothers, 1934), helped inspire a return to Jewish roots among assimilated Jewish intellectuals in America. In his opinion, this movement away from secular ideologies and a return to Jewish sources began slowly in the 1930s, gained momentum after the Second World War, and culminated simultaneously in the writings of Herberg and Heschel. Ludwig Lewisohn, review of *Judaism and Modern Man,* by Will Herberg, in *Congress Weekly* 18 (October 8, 1951): 13–14.

8. See "Under Forty: A Symposium on American Literature and the Younger Generation of American Jews," *Contemporary Jewish Record* (February 1944): 3–37. The symposium was edited by Norman Podhoretz. See, too, Podhoretz's articles, "Jewish Culture and the Intellectuals," *Commentary* 19 (May 1955): 451–457; "The Intellectuals and Jewish Fate," *Midstream* 3 (Winter 1957): 15–23; and Podhoretz's introduction to "Jewishness and the Younger Intellectuals: A Symposium," *Commentary* 31 (April 1961): 306–310. Other important essays written on the subject during the 1950s are Charles Glicksberg's "Religious Attitudes of Jewish Youth," *Congress Weekly* 23 (February 6, 1956): 10–12; and Ben Halpern's "Apologia Contra Rabbines," *Midstream* 11 (Spring 1956): 23–30.

9. For a fuller description of "Hansen's Law," and a citation of its source in Hansen's writings, see chapter 1.

10. See Will Herberg, "Religious Trends in American Jewry," *Judaism* 3 (Summer 1954): 229–240; H. Sherman, "Three Generations," *Jewish Frontier* 21 (July 1954): 12–16; and chapter 6.

11. Eugene Borowitz, *Reform Judaism Today,* Book one. *Reform in the Process of Change* (New York: Behrman House, 1978): 65.

12. Will Herberg, "The Prophetic Faith in an Age of Crisis," *Judaism* 1 (July 1952): 196.

13. Steven Schwarzschild, "Judaism à la Mode," *Menorah Journal* 40 (Spring 1952): 105.

14. Paula Hyman, interview in *Jewish Week,* 17 September 1982.

15. Harold Kushner, "The American-Jewish Experience: A Conservative Perspective," *Judaism* 3 (Summer 1982): 298.

16. Seymour Siegel, "Mordecai Kaplan in Retrospect," *Commentary* 74 (July 1982): 61. Recent essays in the *New York Times* reflect the phenomenon of return associated with this kind of thinking. See Fran Schumer, "A Return to Religion," *New York Times Magazine,* 15 April 1984; and Natalie Gittelson, "American Jews Rediscover Orthodoxy," *New York Times Magazine,* 30 September 1984.

17. The following is a list of some of the leading representatives of the "third generation" of American theologians: (1) Reform—Eugene Borowitz, Lou Silberman, Jakob Petuchowski, Steven Schwarzschild, Samuel Karff, Arnold Wolf, and Bernard Martin, (2) Conservative—Seymour Segel, Fritz Rothschild, Samuel Dresner, Hershel Matt, David Wolf Silverman, Neil Gillman, Richard Rubenstein, and Arthur Cohen, (3) Orthodox—

Shubert Spero, David Hartman, Michael Wyschogrod, Marvin Fox, Irving Greenberg, and Emanuel Rackman.

18. Fackenheim, *Quest,* p. ix.

19. Rubenstein, *After Auschwitz,* p. xi.

20. Eugene Borowitz, *A New Jewish Theology in the Making* (Philadelphia: Westminster Press, 1968): 219.

21. Commenting on the lack of theological activity in Israel, Zwi Werblowsky wrote in 1957: "Perhaps one day, the Jew in Israel will finally come to feel firm and solid ground under his feet. Perhaps this will also enable him to enter into a genuine dialogue with Christianity, without outmoded apologetics and without great disputatiousness and aggressiveness which is, in the last resort, a compensation for fear" ("A Note on the Relations between Judaism and Christianity," *Forum for the Problems of Zionism, Jewry, and the State of Israel: Proceedings of the Jerusalem Ideological Conference* 4 [1959]: 55).

See, too, in this regard, Hartman, *Joy and Responsibility,* chapters, "Torah and Secularism," pp. 54–72; "Halakhah as a Ground for Creating a Shared Spiritual Language," pp. 130–161.

22. Plaut, *Reform Judaism,* p. 351.

23. See Shubert Spero, review of *Ever Since Sinai: A Modern View of Torah,* by Jakob Petuchowski, in *Tradition* 5 (Fall 1962): 102–106; and Spero, "Stirrings in Reform Theology," *The Jewish Observer* 1 (May 1964): 13–15.

24. According to Muffs, David Hartman was the major force behind these meetings (Yochanan Muffs, in conversation, 14 May 1982). See Fackenheim's acknowledgement of Hartman's contribution in *Encounters between Judaism and Modern Philosophy: A Preface to Future Jewish Thought* (New York: Basic Books, 1973): viii. Hartman has helped organize such meetings at Bar Ilan University and elsewhere in Israel. Some of the original group of participants meet on a monthly basis in New York City.

25. Emanuel Rackman, *One Man's Judaism* (Tel Aviv: Greenfield, 1978): 378. See also Charles Liebman, "Left and Right in American Orthodoxy," *Judaism* 15 (Winter 1966): 102–107, and "Orthodoxy in American Jewish Life," *American Jewish Yearbook* 66 (1965): 21–92; Jacob Neusner, "The New Orthodox Left," *Conservative Judaism* 20 (Fall 1965): 10–18; Liebman, "The Orthodox Left: A Reply," *Conservative Judaism* 20 (Winter 1966): 47–52.

26. Emanuel Rackman, "Soloveitchik: On Differing with My Rebbe," *Sh'ma* (March 8, 1985): 65.

27. Rackman, *One Man's Judaism,* p. 378.

28. See, for example, Elliot E. Cohen, "Editorial Statement: An Act of Affirmation," *Commentary* 1 (November 1945): 1–3; Robert Gordis, "The Tasks before Us: A Preface to Our Journal," *Conservative Judaism* 1 (January 1945): 1–8; "Toward a Renascence of Judaism," *Judaism* 1 (January 1952): 3–10.

29. Naomi Cohen, *Not Free to Desist: The American Jewish Committee 1906–1966* (Philadelphia: Jewish Publication Society, 1972): 263–264.

30. Noveck, *Milton Steinberg*, p. 236.

31. Herberg, "Power to Speak?" p. 455. In Europe between the world wars, theologians founded important antiestablishment journals designed to promote "the new thinking" in religious, social, and political thought. Prominent among these were Barth's *Zwischen den Zeiten*, Tillich's *Blätter für religiosen Sozialismus*, and Buber's *Der Jude*.

32. See Gordis, "Genesis of *Judaism*," pp. 390–396; Noveck, *Milton Steinberg*, pp. 322, 256.

33. Steinberg, review of "From Marxism to Judaism," p. 2. See also Noveck, *Milton Steinberg*, p. 253.

34. See, for example, Laura Fermi, *Illustrious Immigrants: The Intellectual Migration from Europe, 1930–1941* (Chicago: University of Chicago Press, 1961); Donald Fleming and Bernard Bailyn, eds., *The Intellectual Migration: Europe and America, 1930–1960* (Cambridge: Harvard University Press, 1969); Lewis Coser, *Refugee Scholars in America: Their Impact and Their Experiences* (New Haven and London: Yale University Press, 1984).

35. See, for example, Peter Berger, *The Heretical Imperative: Contemporary Possibilities of Religious Affirmation* (New York: Doubleday Anchor Books, 1979): 65–66; Alasdair I. C. Heron, *A Century of Protestant Theology* (Philadelphia: Westminster Press, 1980): 68–73.

36. See, for example, William E. Hordern, *A Layman's Guide to Protestant Theology*, 4th ed. (New York: Macmillan, 1970): 73–110.

37. See, for example, Harry Fosdick, *As I See Religion* (New York: Harper & Brothers, 1932).

38. Hordern, *Layman's Guide*, pp. 101–102.

39. Published in 1932, Niebuhr's *Moral Man and Immoral Society: A Study in Ethics and Politics* (New York: Charles Scribner's Sons, 1932) had a stunning effect in American theological circles. According to Patterson, "it carried the same impact in America that Barth's commentary on Romans carried in Europe. . . . No other book in the first third of the twentieth century had a greater impact in American theological circles" (Patterson, *Reinhold Niebuhr*, pp. 32–33). *Moral Man and Immoral Society* was succeeded by *Reflections on the End of an Era* (New York: Charles Scribner's Sons, 1934), and later, *The Nature and Destiny of Man: A Christian Interpretation*, 2 volumes (New York: Charles Scribner's Sons, I: 1941, II: 1943.)

40. Mordecai Kaplan's *Judaism as a Civilization: Toward a Reconstruction of American-Jewish Life* (New York: Macmillan, 1934) was published in 1934, marking a radically new variety of religious liberalism, which quickly replaced in prominence prevailing schools of Jewish thought based on nineteenth-century German idealism.

41. Arthur Cohen, *The Natural and the Supernatural Jew: An Historical and Theological Interpretation* (New York: Pantheon Books, 1962): 232.

42. The younger generation studied the writings of James and Kierkegaard (Hartman and Spero), wrote master's and doctoral theses on Tillich (Rubenstein, Martin, Weiss-Halivni, Rothschild), published articles and books on Barth (Borowitz, Wyschogrod) and Marcel (Gillman), and delivered lengthy papers on Protestant theology at rabbinical conferences (David Wolf Silverman).

43. Wolf, *Rediscovering Judaism,* p. 10.

6. THE NEW JEWISH THEOLOGY IN OUTLINE

1. Siegel, "Will Herberg: Baal Teshuvah," p. 532.

2. Katz, *Jewish Philosophers,* p. 244.

3. Fritz Rothschild, "Herberg as Jewish Theologian," *National Review* 29 (August 1977): 885.

4. Siegel, "Will Herberg: Baal Teshuvah," p. 537.

5. Herberg felt a special kinship with the younger generation, for, like him, many of them were returning to the traditional faith of their forefathers. He began to study and write about the "third generation" in the early 1950s. His studies culminated in *Protestant, Catholic, Jew,* which he dedicated as follows: "*To the Third Generation* upon whose 'return' so much of the future of religion in America depends" (*Protestant, Catholic, Jew* [New York: Doubleday, 1955]). Examples of Herberg's earlier articles on the subject of the "third generation" are: "The Postwar Revival of the Synagogue: Does It Reflect a Religious Reawakening?" *Commentary* 9 (April 1950): 315–325; "The Religious Stirrings on the Campus," *Commentary* 13 (March 1952): 242–244; "Religious Trends in American Jewry," *Judaism* 3 (Summer 1954): 229–240.

6. Will Herberg, *Judaism and Modern Man* (New York: Farrar, Straus & Young, 1951): 39.

7. Herberg, "Prophetic Faith," p. 195.

8. Ibid., pp. 195–196.

9. Herberg, *Judiasm and Modern Man,* p. 6.

10. Will Herberg, "Historicism as Touchstone," *The Christian Century* 77 (March 16, 1960): 313.

11. Ibid.

12. For a description of these concepts see Paul Tillich, *The Protestant Era,* trans. James Luther Adams, abridged edition (Chicago: University of Chicago Press, 1948): 32–51; and Paul Tillich, "Kairos," in *A Handbook of Christian Theology,* ed. Arthur Cohen and Marvin Halverson (Nashville: Abingdon, 1958): 193–197.

13. See, for example, John Stumme, *Socialism in Theological Perspective: A Study of Paul Tillich, 1918–1933* (Ann Arbor: Scholars Press, 1978): 32–38; Ronald Stone, *Paul Tillich's Radical Social Thought* (Atlanta: John Knox

Press, 1980): 45–53; Paul Tillich, *The Socialist Decision,* trans. Franklin Sherman (New York: Harper & Row, 1977): 132–145.

14. See, for example, George Hunsinger, ed. and trans., *Karl Barth and Radical Politics* (Philadelphia: Westminister Press, 1976), and Paul Merkley, *Reinhold Niebuhr: A Political Account* (Montreal: McGill Queen's University Press, 1975).

15. See chapter 1.

16. See Herberg's, "Has Judaism Still Power to Speak?" p. 455, and "Theological Problems," pp. 409–411.

17. Herberg, "Has Judaism Still Power to Speak?," p. 455.

18. Ibid.

19. Herberg, "Theological Problems," p. 426. See, too, Herberg, "From Marxism," p. 32.

20. See, for example, Herberg, *Judaism and Modern Man,* pp. 6–8, and "Rosenzweig's 'Judaism of Personal Existence': A Third Way Between Orthodoxy and Modernism," *Commentary* 6 (December 1950): 541–549.

21. Herberg, "Religious Trends in American Jewry," *Judiasm* 3 (Summer 1954): 235–236. In 1969, Arnold Wolfe wrote in the introduction to *Rediscovering Judaism* that the younger generation of Reform, Conservative, and Orthodox theologians whose writings were represented in the book were typical of their generation.

> For we are not old-fashioned Jews. We have grown up on the American continent (where most of us were born), studied in secular universities (where most of us now teach), assimilated the pragmatism, optimism, and scientism of our century. If we assert traditional doctrine, it is not because we know no alternative. For us, Judaism is not so much a heritage as an achievement. Or, perhaps more accurately, to make it our heritage has become our decisive task (*Rediscovering Judaism,* p. 8).

22. See Herberg, "Rosenzweig's Judaism," pp. 541–549.

23. Herberg, *Judaism and Modern Man,* p. 9.

24. Ibid.

25. Ibid., pp. 8–16.

26. Herberg, "Has Judaism Still Power to Speak?," p. 456.

27. Ibid., p. 451.

28. Will Herberg, "Faith and Secular Learning," in *Christian Faith and Social Action,* ed. John Hutchinson, et al. (New York: Scribners, 1953): 209.

29. Herberg, *Judaism and Modern Man,* p. ix.

30. Herberg, *Judaism and Modern Man,* p. 115. Reinhold Niebuhr wrote often about "Biblical realism" and "Christian realism." Tillich wrote about "Believing realism."

31. For Tillich's understanding of the concept "theonomous era" see his *Systematic Theology* I, pp. 147–159, and *History of Christian Thought,* pp. 530–

535. For Rosenzweig's references to "Johannine age," see *Judaism Despite Christianity,* pp. 14, 21, 35, 46, 66, 157, 160.

   32. Herberg, *Judaism and Modern Man,* pp. 162–163.

   33. See Herberg, "Theological Problems," p. 410.

   34. Herberg, "Theological Problems," p. 415.

   35. Ibid., p. 413. See also *Judaism and Modern Man,* pp. 256–257.

   36. Herberg, "Theological Problems," p. 427.

   37. Herberg, "Athens and Jerusalem," p. 196.

   38. Ibid., pp. 243–261.

   39. Ibid., p. 256.

   40. Herberg attempted to create a theology which would be simultaneously a theology of revelation and grace. He wanted to show that Judaism is a religion of revelation as well as reason, grace, and Law. See, for example, Herberg's "What is Jewish Religion?" pp. 424–426; "Theological Problems," pp. 409–417; *Judaism and Modern Man,* pp. 255–256; "Athens and Jerusalem," p. 183.

   41. See Herberg, "Theological Problems," p. 428; *Judaism and Modern Man,* p. xi.

   42. See, for example, "Theological Problems," p. 410.

   43. Herberg, "Historicism as Touchstone," p. 311.

   44. Arthur Cohen, *The Natural and the Supernatural Jew: An Historical and Theological Interpretation* (New York: Pantheon Books, 1962): 276.

   45. Cohen, *Natural and Supernatural Jew,* p. 277.

   46. Daniel Breslauer, "Will Herberg: Intuitive Spokesman for American Judaism," *Judaism* 27 (Winter 1978): 9.

   47. Herberg, "Theological Problems," p. 427.

7. THE QUESTION OF JEWISH THEOLOGY IN HESCHEL, FACKENHEIM, AND SOLOVEITCHIK

   1. A. J. Heschel, *The Insecurity of Freedom: Essays on Human Existence* (New York: Schocken 1975): 218. See, too, Heschel, "On Prayer," *Conservative Judaism* 25 (Fall 1970): 2, 11.

   2. A. J. Heschel, *God in Search of Man: A Philosophy of Judaism* (New York: Farrar, Straus and Giroux, 1955): 170.

   3. A. J. Heschel, "Teaching Jewish Theology in the Solomon Schechter Day School," *The Synagogue School* 28 (Fall 1969): 20.

   4. See, for example, Heschel's *Israel,* p. 206; "Do Together," p. 134; *God in Search of Man,* pp. 35–36; *Who Is Man?* p. 13; and *Passion for Truth,* p. 301.

   5. Heschel, *Israel,* p. 112.

   6. Heschel, *God in Search of Man,* p. 421.

7. A. J. Heschel, *Who Is Man?* (Stanford: Stanford University Press, 1965): 13–14. For other references of this kind see Heschel's "What We Might Do Together," *Religious Education* 52 (March-April 1967): 134; *Israel: An Echo in Eternity*, 6th printing (New York: Farrar, Straus and Giroux, 1974): 112, 132; and *A Passion for Truth* (New York: Farrar, Straus and Giroux, 1973): 300–301.

8. A. J. Heschel, *Man's Quest for God: Studies in Prayer and Symbolism* (New York: Scribner's, 1954): 95.

9. Heschel, "Teaching Jewish Theology," p. 7. For Heschel, "Jewish thinking," can only be adequately understood in terms of a dialectical pattern involving contrasting properties. He tried to illustrate these poles of Jewish thinking in a number of ways. He referred to them as the Hebraic (biblical) and Hellenistic (Greco-Germanic) in *God in Search of Man* and *Man Is Not Alone;* the Sephardic and Ashkenazic in *The Earth is the Lord's;* the ways of Rabbi Ishmael and Rabbi Akiva in *Torah min ha-shamayim b'espaku-laria shel ha-dorot*, 2 vols. (London: Soncino, 1962–1965); and the ways of Rabbi Mendele of Kotzk and the Baal Shem Tov in *A Passion for Truth.* See *God in Search of Man*, pp. 102, 341; *Man's Quest for God*, p. 65; *Insecurity of Freedom*, p. 136.

10. Heschel, *God in Search of Man*, p. 320.

11. Heschel, "Teaching Jewish Theology," pp. 4–6.

12. Heschel, *Insecurity of Freedom*, p. 217. See, too, *God in Search of Man*, pp. 321–322.

13. See, for example, *God in Search of Man*, pp. 322–335. For Heschel's conviction that the Bible contains a coherent philosophical outlook, see Edmond La B. Cherbonnier, "A. J. Heschel and the Philosophy of the Bible: Mystic or Rationalist?" *Commentary* 27 (January 1959): 23–29, and "Heschel as a Religious Thinker," *Conservative Judaism* 23 (Fall 1968): 25–39.

14. Heschel, "Teaching Jewish Theology," pp. 66–67.

15. Heschel, *Man's Quest for God*, p. 95.

16. Heschel, *God in Search of Man*, pp. 14, 24, 321–322.

17. Cherbonnier, "Religious Thinker," p. 25.

18. Heschel, *God in Search of Man*, p. 23. See Granfield's interview with Heschel, Patrick Granfield, *Theologians at Work* (New York: Macmillan, 1967): 80.

19. Heschel, *Insecurity of Freedom*, p. 4.

20. Ibid., p. 116; *God in Search of Man*, pp. 1–20.

21. Heschel, *God in Search of Man*, p. 4.

22. Ibid., pp. 422–423.

23. Ibid., p. 8.

24. Heschel, "Do Together," p. 137.

25. See Heschel's *God in Search of Man*, p. 5. *Insecurity of Freedom*, pp. 115–126; *Passion for Truth*, p. 86; and Edward Kaplan, "Language and

Reality in Abraham J. Heschel's Philosophy of Religion," *Journal of the American Academy of Religion* 41 (March 1973): 9.

26. Heschel, *God in Search of Man,* p. 18. Heschel is typical of religious existentialists in rejecting the identification of Judaism with rationalist philosophy. He thought nothing, however, of identifyinq Judaism with existentialist philosophy (Kierkegaard) and phenomenological methods (Husserl). See, for example, *God in Search of Man,* pp. 18–20; and Heschel's introduction to the English edition of *The Prophets* (New York: Harper & Row, 1962): pp. xiii-xix.

27. Heschel, *Who Is Man?,* pp. 13–14.

28. Heschel, *God in Search of Man,* p. 19.

29. Ibid., p. 20.

30. See, for example, Heschel, *Man Is Not Alone,* pp. 126–128, 241; *God in Search of Man,* pp. 126–127; Granfield, *Theologians,* p. 80. Like Buber and Rosenzweig, Barth and Tillich, Heschel placed great stress on the role of divine initiative (Grace) in the acquisition of religious knowledge and faith. Heschel's title for his 1955 book, *God in Search of Man* reflects this. It may have been influenced by the title of the 1935 work, *God's Search for Man: Sermons by Karl Barth and Eduard Thurneysen* (Edinburgh: T & T Clark, 1935).

31. See, for example, Paul Tillich, *Protestant Era,* pp. 83–93; and *Systematic Theology* I, pp. 18–28. Although Heschel's form of "question and answer" theology is similar in some respects to that of Tillich, it was "independently conceived" (Fritz Rothschild, "Architect and Herald of a New Theology," *Conservative Judaism* 28 [Fall 1973]: 56–57).

32. Heschel, *God in Search of Man,* p. 4.

33. Heschel, *God in Search of Man,* p. 15.

34. Fackenheim, *Quest,* p. 121.

35. Ibid., pp. 100, 106, 107.

36. Ibid., p. 5.

37. Ibid., p. 127.

38. Fackenheim, *God's Presence,* pp. 30–31; *The Jewish Return into History: Reflections in the Age of Auschwitz and a New Jerusalem* (New York: Schocken Books, 1978): 10, 48.

39. Fackenheim, *Quest,* p. 56.

40. Ibid., pp. 7, 58.

41. Emil Fackenheim, "Liberalism and Reform Judaism," *Central Conference of American Rabbis Journal* No. 21 (April 1958): 59. In regard to Fackenheim's neo-orthodoxy, see Fackenheim, *Quest,* pp. 4, 21; *Jewish Return,* p. 8; and Michael Meyer, "Judaism after Auschwitz: The Religious Thought of Emil L. Fackenheim," *Commentary* 52 (June 1972).

42. See Fackenheim, *Quest,* pp. 16, 34, 54, 57, 100, 172, 204, 228 and *God's Presence,* pp. 20–25.

43. See, for example, Emil Fackenheim, "The Possibility of the Universe

in Al-Farabi, Ibn Sina, and Maimonides" *Proceedings of the American Academy of Jewish Research* 16 (1947): 39–70; Fackenheim, "Martin Buber's Concept of Revelation" in *The Philosophy of Martin Buber,* ed. Maurice Friedman and Arthur Schilpp (LaSalle, Illinois: Open Court, 1967): 274. For Heschel's interpretation of Maimonides, see A. J. Heschel, *Maimonides: A Biography* (New York: Farrar, Straus and Giroux, 1982). According to Lichtenstein, Soloveitchik was interested in showing that Maimonidean scholarship had erred in seeing Maimonides as a confirmed Aristotelian rationalist. See Aharon Lichtenstein, "R. Joseph Soloveitchik," in Noveck, *Jewish Thinkers,* p. 285. See also Joseph Soloveitchik, "The Lonely Man of Faith," *Tradition* 7 (Summer 1965): 32–33.

44. Fackenheim, *Quest,* pp. 98–99.

45. See, for example, *Quest for Past and Future: Essays in Jewish Theology; God's Presence in History: Jewish Affirmations and Philosophical Reflections; Encounters Between Judaism and Modern Philosophy: A Preface to Future Jewish Thought; The Jewish Return into History: Reflections in the Age of Auschwitz and a New Jerusalem; To Mend the World: Foundations of Future Jewish Thought.*

46. Emil Fackenheim, *To Mend the World: Foundations of Future Jewish Thought* (New York: Schocken, 1982): 5.

47. Fackenheim, *To Mend the World,* p. 4. Whereas Heschel and Soloveitchik's writings are often considered "poetic" and "homiletic," Fackenheim's are generally held to be more "philosophical." His writings appear to be more systematic and philosophically sophisticated than theirs. If this is indeed the case, the reason may be that Fackenheim was a professor of philosophy at a secular university. Working in a strictly academic environment, with a great deal of competition within his profession, he had to be rigorous in expressing his ideas and demonstrating his theological position. It has been otherwise with Heschel and Soloveitchik. They have taught theology, rather than strict philosophy, at rabbinical seminaries where theology is not held in high regard, competition in their field is lacking, and rigorous argument is reserved for talmudic and related fields of study.

48. Fackenheim, *Quest,* p. 99.

49. Fackenheim maintained that a pure religious existentialism devoid of all structure would lead to anarchism, for it would be unable to distinguish between authentic and inauthentic modes of Jewish thought. The notion of "essence" is important, he argues, as a heuristic principle. See *Quest,* pp. 13–14.

50. Fackenheim, *Quest,* p. 14.

51. Fackenheim, *Jewish Return,* pp. 16–19.

52. Ibid., p. 10, *Quest,* p. 16.

53. See Fackenheim, *Quest,* pp. 16–17, note 17, 318; *To Mend the World,* p. 16.

54. Fackenheim, *Quest,* p. 106.

55. Fackenheim first presented this position in his reviews of Heschel's

Man Is Not Alone in *Judaism* I (January 1952): 85–89 and *God in Search of Man* in *Conservative Judaism* 15 (Fall 1960): 50–53.

56. Fackenheim, review of *God in Search of Man*, p. 50.

57. Ibid., p. 51; Fackenheim, review of *Man Is Not Alone*, pp. 85–86.

58. Fackenheim, review of *God in Search of Man*, p. 50.

59. Fackenheim, *Quest*, p. 208.

60. See Emil Fackenheim, "Hermann Cohen: After Fifty Years," *Leo Baeck Memorial Lecture* 12 (New York: Leo Baeck Institute, 1969): 1–27; "Schelling's Conception of Positive Philosophy," *Review of Metaphysics* 7 (June 1954): 566; *Encounters*, p. 228.

61. Fackenheim, *God's Presence*, pp. 48–49.

62. Fackenheim, *Quest*, p. 17; *God's Presence*, p. 31.

63. Fackenheim, *Jewish Return*, pp. 43, 48.

64. See Fackenheim, *Jewish Return*, pp. xi–xii, 43, and "Kant and Radical Evil," *University of Toronto Quarterly* 23 (July 1954): 339, 353.

65. Fackenheim, *Quest*, p. 101.

66. Fackenheim, *Quest* p. 83.

67. Ibid., p. 11; and *Jewish Return*, p. 6.

68. See Fackenheim, *Encounters*, pp. 130–134.

69. Fackenheim, *Quest*, p. 170.

70. Ibid., p. 6.

71. Joseph Soloveitchik, *Reflections of the Rav: Lessons in Jewish Thought*, ed. Abraham R. Besdin (Jerusalem: World Zionist Organization, 1979): 23.

72. Joseph Soloveitchik, *The Halakhic Mind: An Essay on Jewish Tradition and Modern Thought* (New York: Free Press, 1986). Most commentators on the writings of Soloveitchik agree that it is difficult at present to adequately assess his theological views. The reasons commonly given for this are the following: (1) Soloveitchik has reportedly written a great deal, but has published little, therefore, "the largest part of his intellectual output is simply not available for assessment" (David Singer and Moshe Sokol, "Joseph Soloveitchik: Lonely Man of Faith" *Modern Judaism* 2 [October 1982]: 229, 231–232); (2) the consideration of particular essays is made difficult because they tend to be fragmentary, disjointed, and inconsistent (Pinchas H. Peli, introduction to *On Repentance in the Thought and Oral Discourses of Rabbi Joseph B. Soloveitchik*, edited and reconstructed by Pinchas H. Peli, English ed. [Jerusalem: Orot, 1980]: 22); (3) although in recent years more of Soloveitchik's writings have appeared in print, "the cumulative effect of the recent publications is to cast Soloveitchik in the role of neither a systematic theologian nor philosopher, but of a deeply serious and anguished religious personality whose later publications do not resolve inconsistencies in his earlier writings, but only repeat them or render them more acute" (Hillel Goldberg, "Soloveitchik's Lonely Quest," *Midstream* 28 [November 1982]: 31–32).

73. See Robert Goldy, "The Lonely Man of Faith as Theologian," (unpublished manuscript, 1979).

74. Soloveitchik, "Man of Faith," p. 44.

75. Ibid., pp. 5–6.

76. Ibid., p. 44.

77. Ibid., p. 6.

78. Ibid., p. 9.

79. Ibid., p. 10.

80. Ibid.

81. Ibid.

82. Typical of neo-orthodox theologians (viz., Buber, Barth, Tillich, Niebuhr, Herberg, Fackenheim, and Heschel), Soloveitchik distinguishes between the "Man of Faith," and the "Man of Religion," and takes a critical, confrontational stance in relation to organized religion. In "The Sacred and the Profane," for example, he characterized American Judaism in terms of William James's notion of the "religion of the happy-minded." Modern religion, Soloveitchik argued, is sold to the nonbeliever as a "drug" or "opiate," promising worldly happiness while at the same time it robs the religious act of its vitality and becomes what Kierkegaard called "technical wisdom." In "The Lonely Man of Faith" Soloveitchik distinguished between the man of religion—modern, secular, "Majestic Man," (or "Adam I") and the man of authentic religiosity, the "Man of Faith," (or "Adam II"). The religious community is created to serve the selfish, egoistic needs of secular man. The man of religion has forgotten how to pray. His community is a "utilitarian, work-community." The faith community, on the other hand, is "existential," "covenantal," and "halakhic." It is a truly "prayerful" community. See "The Sacred and the Profane," pp. 4–5; "Man of Faith," p. 56; and *Shiurei Harav: A Conspectus of the Public Lecitures of Rabbi Joseph B. Soloveitchik,* ed. Joseph Epstein (New York: Hamevaser, Yeshiva University, 1974): 75–80.

83. Lou Silberman, "Theology in North America," p. 54.

84. Soloveitchik, "Man of Faith," pp. 10, 35, 59–67.

85. See Heschel and Fackenheim, this chapter.

86. See, for example, Soloveitchik, "Man of Faith," pp. 56–65.

87. Ibid., p. 63.

88. Soloveitchik, "Man of Faith," pp. 12–15, 18.

89. Ibid., p. 56.

90. See, for example, Paul Tillich, *The Interpretation of History,* trans. N. A. Rasetzki and Elsa L. Talmey (New York: Charles Scribner's Sons, 1936): 77–122.

91. Joseph Soloveitchik, "Man of Faith," pp. 15, 63.

92. Ibid., pp. 62–67.

93. Ibid., pp. 19–23, 38, 56–59, 62–67.

94. See, for example, David L. Mueller, *Karl Barth,* Makers of the Mod-

ern Theological Mind Series (Waco, Texas: Word Books, 1972): 35–37; Herbert Hartwell, *The Theology of Karl Barth: An Introduction* (Philadelphia: Westminster Press, 1964): 53–56.

95. See, for example, Alexander J. McKelway, *The Systematic Theology of Paul Tillich: A Review and Analysis* (New York: Delta Books, 1964): 45–49; John P. Clayton, "Questioning, Answering, and Tillich's Concept of Correlation," in *Kairos and Logos: Studies in the Roots and Implications of Tillich's Theology,* ed. John J. Carey (Cambridge, Mass.: The North American Paul Tillich Society, 1978): 135–157.

96. Soloveitchik has adopted Barthian notions of revelation, grace, the faith community, and, according to some commentators, a Barthian model of biblical exegesis. Lou Silberman has written in regard to Barth: "When reading Soloveitchik, one is struck almost at once with the programmatic similarity of these two men. Essentially, they theologize out of man's existential situation, from biblical text ("Theology in North America," p. 52).

In a recent article on Soloveitchik, Singer and Sokol have written: "Soloveitchik was aware of Barth's works at an early date and admiringly referred to them. Maimonides and Barth offer him models of how to use the biblical text as a spring board for an intellectually sophisticated discussion of the human condition. That, precisely, is what we have in 'The Lonely Man of Faith' " ("Joseph Soloveitchik," p. 240).

97. Soloveitchik, "Man of Faith," pp. 44, 59–63.

98. Ibid., pp. 44–45, 60–62.

99. Ibid., p. 65.

100. Ibid., pp. 62–63.

101. Ibid.

102. Ibid., p. 62.

103. Ibid.

104. Ibid.

105. There are many commentaries on Soloveitchik's writings that refer to the influence on Soloveitchik of phenomenological, existentialist and Protestant neo-orthodox schools of thought. See, for example, Morris Sosevsky, "The Lonely Man of Faith Confronts the Ish Ha-Halakhah: An Analysis of the Critique of Rabbi Joseph B. Soloveitchik's Philosophical Writings," *Tradition* 16 (Fall 1976): 85; Ruth Birnbaum, "The Man of Dialogue and the Man of Halakhah," *Judaism* 26 (Winter 1977): 53–57; Z'vi Kurzweil, "Universalism in the Philosophy of Rabbi Joseph B. Soloveitchik," *Judaism* 13 (Fall 1982): 463, 467, 469–470; Edward Kaplan, "The Religious Philosophy of Rabbi Joseph Soloveitchik," *Tradition* 14 (Fall 1973): 45–47; Eugene Borowitz, "A Theology of Modern Orthodoxy: Rabbi Joseph B. Soloveitchik," in *Choices in Modern Jewish Thought: A Partisan Guide* (New York: Behrman House, 1983): 220–222, 224–231.

106. The essay, "The Lonely Man of Faith," is a description of "the man of halakha" because "the man of faith," as defined by Soloveitchik, is also

a "man of halakha." This is true for the following reasons: (1) the community of which "the man of faith" is a member is a "covenantal-halakhic" community; that is, its members are committed and covenanted to God as defined by the principles of halakha (see, for example, "Man of Faith," pp. 30, 33, 40, 43); (2) as a member of the "covenantal-halakhic" community, "the man of faith" has as his divinely ordained task, the duty to bring the redeeming message of the Halakha to modern, secular man ("Man of Faith," p. 67). If successful, the result of the "man of faith's" activity will pave the way for what Tillich has called a "theonomous" era in which human heteronomy (commitment to God) and human autonomy (commitment to creative, human freedom) will be united. The halakha, Soloveitchik maintains, has a monistic approach to reality. According to it, "there is only one world—not divisible into secular and hallowed sectors." As such, "the task of covenantal man is in uniting the two communities into one community where man is both the creative, free agent, and the obedient servant of God" ("Man of Faith," p. 51).

107. It is with this in mind that commentators have maintained that Soloveitchik's theology is "derived from" (Rackman, "Orthodox Judaism," p. 548), "speaks from" (Katz, *Jewish Philosophers*, p. 216), and theologizes "from within the fixed structures of Halakha" (Birnbaum, "Man of Dialogue," p. 52).

108. Emanuel Rackman, "Orthodox Judaism," p. 548.

109. Hillel Goldberg, "Soloveitchik," p. 31.

110. David Singer and Moshe Sokol, "Joseph Soloveitchik," p. 260.

111. Eugene Borowitz, *New Theology*, p. 169; see *Choices*, p. 223. See also in this regard Lichtenstein, "R. Joseph Soloveitchik," pp. 296; Sosevsky, "Soloveitchik's Philosophical Writings," p. 86; Peli, *On Repentance*, pp. 33, 47; Singer and Sokol; "Joseph Soloveitchik," pp. 232, 260; Birnbaum, "Man of Dialogue," p. 60; Epstein, *Shiurei Harav*, pp. 3–4; Peli, "Repentant Man: A High Level in Rabbi Soloveitchk's Typeology of Man," *Tradition* 18 (Summer 1980): 143.

112. Joseph Epstein, ed., *Shurei Harav*, p. 56.

113. Joseph Soloveitchik, *Halakhic Man*, p. 5. To avoid possible confusion, it ought to be mentioned that "Halakhic Man" first appeared in 1944 as a long essay published in the journal *Talpiot*, vol. 1, nos. 3–4, pp. 651–735. In 1983, an English translation of the essay appeared in book form as *Halakhic Man*.

114. Ibid., p. 137.

115. Joseph Soloveitchik, "Man of Faith," pp. 5–10.

116. Lawrence Kaplan, preface to *Halakhic Man*, pp. vii–ix.

117. Eugene Borowitz, *New Theology*, p. 161.

118. Arnold Wolfe, "On My Mind," *Sh'ma* (September 19, 1975): 295.

119. Lou Silberman, "Theology in North America," p. 54.

120. Eliezer Berkovits, personal conversation, May 1978.

121. Hillel Goldberg, "Soloveitchik," p. 32.

122. Ibid.

123. David Hartman, "The Breakdown of Tradition and the Quest for Renewal: Reflections on Three Jewish Responses to Modernity, Part 1: J. B. Soloveitchik": *Forum* 37 (Spring 1980): 14–15. See, too, David Hartman, *Joy and Responsibility,* pp. 199–201; and Goldy, "Man of Faith as Theologian," pp. 41–46.

124. See section II, this chapter.

125. Hartman, *Joy and Responsibility,* p. 228.

126. See section II, this chapter; chapter 6; Hartman, *Joy and Responsibility,* pp. 1–14; and Heschel, *Israel: An Echo of Eternity.*

127. Some of Soloveitchik's writings have been published since 1975 in Israel by the World Zionist Organization, The Jewish Agency, Mosad Rav Kook, and the Tal Orot Institute. His *Halakhic Man* was published in 1983 by the Jewish Publication Society of America and the Paulist Press. *The Halakhic Mind* was published in New York and London by the Free Press, a division of Macmillan Company.

128. Joseph Soloveitchik, "Confrontation," *Tradition* 6 (Spring/Summer 1964): 17–29.

129. Rackman, "On Differing with My Rebbe," p. 65.

130. Ibid. See also chapter 5.

8. FROM WHENCE WE HAVE COME

1. Steinberg's comment appeared on the dust jacket of Herberg's *Judaism and Modern Man.* Steinberg died a year before the book appeared in print. He read it, however, in manuscript form as it was being written between 1948 and 1950. See Noveck, *Milton Steinberg,* pp. 217–218.

2. The symposium, "Will Herberg Redivivus," took place at Drew University in Madison, New Jersey, October 28–29, 1982. The Herberg archives are located in the Drew University library. Janet Gnall has written a doctoral dissertation on Herberg entitled, "Will Herberg, a Jewish Theologian: A Biblical-Existential Approach to Religion," (Drew University, 1983). Two collections of Herberg's essays have been published: *Faith Enacted as History: Essays in Biblical Theology,* ed. Bernhard Anderson (Philadelphia: Westminster Press, 1976), and *From Marxism to Judaism: Selected Essays of Will Herberg,* ed. David G. Dalin (New York: Markus Wiener Publishing, 1988). Biographical material on Herberg's life and thought appears in John Diggin's *Up from Communism* (New York: Harper and Row, 1975). Harry J. Ausmus has written two recent studies on Herberg's life and thought. See Ausmus, *Will Herberg: A Bio-Bibliography* (Westport, Connecticut: Greenwood Press, 1986), and *Will Herberg: From Right to Right* (Chapel Hill & London: University of North Carolina Press, 1987).

3. During his lifetime, Heschel was an important influence on Protestant thinkers, especially Reinhold Niebuhr and Paul Tillich, on Martin
Luther King, Jr., and on the civil rights and peace movements. An advisor
to popes John XXIII and Paul VI, Heschel influenced the drafting of the
Ecumenical Council's "Schema on the Jews."

4. Heschel's *Yahrzeit* is observed at the home of Mrs. Sylvia Heschel in
New York City. Scholars gather at this event to read papers on a variety
of topics dedicated to Heschel's memory. In 1983, conferences devoted to
Heschel's life and work were held at the Jewish Theological Seminary, the
College of Saint Benedict, Saint Joseph, Minnesota, at a Quaker retreat in
New York State, and at the University of Portland. By the early 1980s every
university in Israel was teaching Heschel as part of the mainstream of Jewish
thought. See Pinchas Peli, "Heschel and the Hassidic Tradition," in *Prayer
and Politics: The Twin Poles of Abraham Joshua Heschel,* ed. Joshua Stampfer
(Portland: Institute for Judiac Studies, 1985), p. 74. After Heschel's death,
most of his works were republished by Farrar, Straus and Giroux: *The
Sabbath* (1975), *Man Is Not Alone* (1976), *God in Search of Man* (1976), and
The Earth Is the Lord's (1978). The company also published a collection of
his sayings as *The Wisdom of Heschel,* ed. Ruth Marcus Goodhill (1975), and
an English translation of Heschel's *Maimonides: A Biography* (1982). In 1983
Samuel Dresner edited a collection of Heschel's writings, *I Asked for Wonder:
A Spiritual Anthology* (New York: Crossroads, 1983), and another in 1985,
The Circle of the Baal Shem Tov: Studies in Hasidism by A. J. Heschel (Chicago:
University of Chicago Press, 1985). Two studies of Heschel's life and
thought appeared at the end of the 1970s: Byron Sherwin, *Abraham Joshua
Heschel,* Makers of Contemporary Theology Series (Atlanta: John Knox,
1979), and Harold Kasimov, *Divine-Human Encounter: A Study of Abraham
Joshua Heschel* (Washington, D.C.: University Press of America, 1979). In
1985 two important works on Heschel appeared: John Merkle, *The Genesis
of Faith: The Depth Theology of Abraham Joshua Heschel* (New York: Macmillan,
1985), and John Merkle, ed., *Abraham Joshua Heschel: Exploring His Life and
Thought* (New York: Macmillan, 1985). Essays on Heschel's work appear
regularly. Some worth noting are the following: Nathan Rotenstreich, "On
Prophetic Consciousness," *The Journal of Religion* 54 (July 1974): 185–198;
Edward Kaplan, "Mysticism and Despair in Abraham J. Heschel's Religious
Thought," *Journal of Religion* 57 (January 1977): 33–47; Steven Katz, "A.
J. Heschel and Hasidism," *The Journal of Jewish Studies* 31 (Spring 1980):
82–104; David Hartman, "The Breakdown of Tradition and the Quest for
Renewal: Reflections on Three Jewish Responses to Modernity, Part 4:
Abraham Joshua Heschel," *Forum* 39 (Fall 1980): 61–75.

5. Rackman, "Orthodox Judaism," pp. 545–550.

6. See, for example, *In Aloneness, in Togetherness: A Selection of Hebrew
Writings of Rabbi Joseph B. Soloveitchik* (Hebrew), ed. Pinchas Peli (Jerusalem:
Orot, 1976); *Halakhic Man* (Philadelphia: Jewish Publication Society, 1983);

The Halakhic Mind (New York: Free Press, 1986); *The Man of Halakha—
Hidden and Revealed* [Hebrew], (Jerusalem: World Zionist Organization,
1979); *On Repentance in the Thought and Oral Discourses of Rabbi Joseph B.
Soloveitchik,* ed. Pinchas Peli (Jerusalem: Orot, Hebrew, 1975; English,
1980); *The Rav Speaks: Five Addresses by Rabbi Joseph Soloveitchik* (Jerusalem:
Orot, Hebrew 1974; English, 1984); *Reflections of the Rav: Lessons in Jewish
Thought,* ed. Abraham R. Besdin (Jerusalem: World Zionist Organization,
1979); *Shiurei Harav: A Conspectus of the Public Lectures of Rabbi Joseph B.
Soloveitchik,* ed. Joseph Epstein (New York: Hamevaser-Yeshiva University,
1974). See chapter 7 for a partial list of commentaries.

7. See Eisen, *Chosen,* pp. 176–180. Although many rabbis and religious
thinkers continue to turn to sociology and ideology rather than theology
for answers to religious questions, Jewish theology continues to play an
important role—although, of course, not the only one—in American Jewish
intellectual life.

8. Although a Canadian citizen, and therefore strictly a North American, Fackenheim is considered to be an "American Jewish theologian" in
the United States. Most of his writings have been published in the United
States, and he continues to lecture here at academic conferences, rabbinical
conventions, synagogues, and Hillel Foundations.

9. Soloveitchik's reasons for opposing interfaith dialogue of a theological nature are to be found in his essay, "Confrontation," pp. 21–29. The
Orthodox theologian Eliezer Berkovits also opposes it. See his "Judaism in
the Post-Christian Age," *Judaism* 15 (Winter 1966): 74–84; and "Facing the
Truth," *Judaism* 27 (Summer 1978): 324–326.

10. See, for example, Michael Oppenheim, "Eliezer Schweid: A Phi-
losophy of Return," *Judaism* 35 (Winter 1986): 66–77; and David Hartman's
Joy and Responsibility and *A Living Covenant: The Innovative Spirit in Traditional
Judaism* (New York: The Free Press, 1985).

11. Hartman, *Living Covenant,* p. ix.

12. Norbert Samuelson, "Introduction: The Academy for Jewish Philosophy," in *Studies in Jewish Philosophy* I (Melrose Park, Penn.: Academy
for Jewish Philosophy, 1980): 5.

13. Steven Katz, "Jewish Philosophy in the 1980s: A Diagnosis and Prescription," in Samuelson, p. 33.

14. Michael Wyschogrod, *The Body of Faith: Judaism as Corporeal Election*
(Minneapolis: The Seabury Press, 1983).

15. See Harold Kushner, *When Bad Things Happen to Good People* (New
York: Schocken, 1981).

16. See David Novak and Norbert Samuelson, eds., *Creation and the End
of Days: Judaism and Scientific Cosmology,* Proceedings of the 1984 Meeting
of the Academy for Jewish Philosophy (New York: University Press of
America, 1986); and Norbert Samuelson, ed., *Studies in Jewish Philosophy,*

Collected Essays of the Academy for Jewish Philosophy, 1980–1985 (New York: University Press of America, 1987).

17. See Carol P. Christ and Judith Plaskow, eds., *Womanspirit Rising: A Feminist Reader in Religion* (San Francisco: Harper and Row, 1979) and Susannah Heschel, ed., *On Being a Jewish Feminist: A Reader* (New York: Schocken, 1983).

18. Plaskow, "The Right Question is Theological," in *Jewish Feminist,* p. 223.

19. Heschel, introduction to *Jewish Feminist,* p. xxxii.

20. Many Jewish feminists deal with theological issues from the perspective of disciplines other than theology, namely, literature, history, psychology, sociology, Bible, or Talmud. However, there is a growing cadre of Jewish feminist theologians with advanced degrees in theology, philosophy, and religion, and who make a vocation of teaching and writing theology. Included among the latter are Judith Plaskow, Arthur Waskow, Rita Gross, Joanna Katz, Susannah Heschel, and Arthur Green.

SOURCES CITED

A. BOOKS

Agus, Jacob. *Guideposts in Modern Judaism: An Analysis of Current Trends in Jewish Thought.* New York: Bloch, 1954.

———. *Modern Philosophies of Judaism: A Study of Recent Jewish Philosophies of Religion.* New York: Behrman, 1941.

Ausmus, Harry J. *Will Herberg: A Bio-Bibliography.* Westport, Connecticut: Greenwood Press, 1986.

———. *Will Herberg: From Right to Right.* Chapel Hill & London: University of North Carolina Press, 1987.

Barrett, William. *Irrational Man: A Study in Existential Philosophy.* New York: Doubleday Anchor, 1958.

Barth, Karl, *Church Dogmatics.* Eds. G. W. Bromiley and T. F. Torrance. Trans. G. W. Bromiley. 4 vols. Edinburgh: T & T Clark, 1936–1969.

———. *Protestant Theology in the Nineteenth Century: Its Background and History.* Valley Forge, Pennsylvania: Judson Press, 1972.

Barth, Karl and Eduard Thurneysen. *God's Search for Man: Sermons by Karl Barth and Eduard Thurneysen.* Edinburgh: T & T Clark, 1935.

Berger, Peter. *The Heretical Imperative: Contemporary Possibilities of Religious Affirmation.* New York: Doubleday Anchor, 1979.

Biale, David. *Gershom Scholem, Kabbalah and Counter-History.* Boston: Harvard University Press, 1982.

Borowitz, Eugene. *Choices in Modern Jewish Thought: A Partisan's Guide,* New York: Behrman, 1983.

———. *A New Jewish Theology in the Making.* Philadelphia: Westminster Press, 1968.

———. *Reform Judaism Today.* Book one, *Reform in the Process of Change.* Book two, *What We Believe.* Book three, *How We Live.* New York: Behrman, 1978.

Buber, Martin. *At the Turning: Three Addresses on Judaism.* New York: Farrar, Straus and Young, 1952.

———. *The Writings of Martin Buber.* Ed. Will Herberg. Cleveland and New York: Meridian, 1956.

Carey, John J., ed. *Kairos and Logos: Studies in the Roots and Implications of Tillich's Theology.* Cambridge, Massachusetts: The North American Paul Tillich Society, 1978.

Christ, Carol P. and Judith Plaskow, eds. *Womanspirit Rising: A Feminist Reader in Religion.* San Francisco: Harper and Row, 1979.

Cohen, Arthur. *The Natural and The Supernatural Jew: An Historical and Theological Interpretation.* New York: Pantheon, 1962.

———, ed. *Arguments and Doctrines: A Reader of Jewish Thinking in the Aftermath.* New York: Harper & Row, 1970.

Cohen, Arthur and Marvin Halverson, eds. *A Handbook of Christian Theology.* Nashville: Abingdon, 1958.

Cohen, Morris Raphael. *A Dreamer's Journey: The Autobiography of Morris Raphael Cohen.* 2nd ed. New York: Arno Press, 1975.

Cohen, Naomi. *Not Free to Desist: The American Jewish Committee 1906–1966.* Philadelphia: Jewish Publication Society, 1972.

Cohon, Samuel S. *Daybook of Services at the Altar as Lived by Samuel S. Cohon, 1888–1959*. Los Angeles: Times Mirror Press, 1978.

Coser, Lewis A. *Refugee Scholars in America: Their Impact and Their Experiences*. New Haven and London: Yale University Press, 1984.

Davis, Moshe. *The Emergence of Conservative Judaism*. Philadelphia: Jewish Publication Society, 1963.

Diggins, John. *Up From Communism*. New York: Harper & Row, 1975.

Eisen, Arnold. *The Chosen People in America: A Study in Jewish Religious Ideology*. Bloomington: Indiana University Press, 1983.

Eisenstein, Ira. Foreword to *Contemporary Jewish Philosophy*, by William Kaufman. New York: Reconstructionist Press and Behrman, 1976.

Fackenheim, Emil. *Encounters between Judaism and Modern Philosophy: A Preface to Future Jewish Thought*. New York: Basic Books, 1973.

———. *God's Presence in History: Jewish Affirmations and Philosophical Reflections*. New York: Harper Torchbooks, 1970.

———. *The Jewish Return into History: Reflections in the Age of Auschwitz and a New Jerusalem*. New York: Schocken, 1978.

———. *Quest for Past and Future: Essays in Jewish Theology*. Boston: Beacon Press, 1968.

———. *To Mend the World: Foundations of Future Jewish Thought*. New York: Schocken, 1982.

Fermi, Laura. *Illustrious Immigrants: The Intellectual Migration from Europe, 1930–1941*. Chicago: University of Chicago Press, 1961.

Fleming, Donald, and Bernard Bailyn, eds. *The Intellectual Migration: Europe and America, 1930–1960*. Cambridge: Harvard University Press, 1969.

Fosdick, Harry. *As I See Religion*. New York: Harper & Brothers, 1932.

Friedman, Maurice. *Martin Buber: The Life of Dialogue*. New York: Harper & Brothers, 1960. Originally published by the University of Chicago Press, 1955.

Friedman, Theodore, and Robert Gordis, eds. *Jewish Life in America*. New York: Horizon, 1955.

Ginzberg, Eli. *Keeper of the Law: Louis Ginzberg*. Philadelphia: Jewish Publication Society, 1966.

Glatzer, Nahum. *Franz Rosenzweig: His Life and Thought*. New York: Schocken, 1953.

Gnall, Janet. "Will Herberg, a Jewish Theologian: A Biblical-Existential Approach to Religion." Ph.D. dissertation, Drew University, 1983.

Goldy, Robert. "The Lonely Man of Faith as Theologian." Unpublished manuscript, 1979.

Gordis, Robert. *Faith for Moderns*. New York: Bloch, 1960.

Granfield, Patrick. *Theologians at Work*. New York: Macmillan, 1967.

Guttman, Julius. *Philosophies of Judaism: A History of Jewish Philosophy from Biblical Times to Franz Rosenzweig*. Second printing. Trans. David W. Silverman. Intro. R. J. Zwi Werblowsky. New York: Schocken, 1976.

Hansen, Marcus Lee. *The Immigrant in American History*. Cambridge: Harvard University Press, 1940.

———. *The Problem of the Third Generation Immigrant*. Illinois: Augustana Historical Society, 1938.

Hartman, David. *Joy and Responsibility: Israel, Modernity, and the Renewal of Judaism*. Jerusalem: Ben-zvi Posner/Shalom Hartman Institute, 1978.

———. *A Living Covenant: The Innovative Spirit in Traditional Judaism*. New York: The Free Press, 1985.

Hartwell, Herbert. *The Theology of Karl Barth: An Introduction*. Philadelphia: Westminster Press, 1964.

Herberg, Will. *Faith Enacted as History: Essays in Biblical Theology*. Edited with an introduction by Bernard W. Anderson. Philadelphia: Westminster Press, 1976.

———. *From Marxism to Judaism: Selected Essays of Will Herberg.* Edited with an introduction by David G. Dalin. New York: Markus Wiener Publishing, 1988.

———. *Judaism and Modern Man.* New York: Farrar, Straus & Young, 1951.

———. *Protestant, Catholic, Jew.* New York: Doubleday, 1955.

Heron, Alasdair I. C. *A Century of Protestant Theology.* Philadelphia: Westminster Press, 1980.

Heschel. Abraham J. *Between God and Man: An Interpretation of Judaism from the Writings of Abraham J. Heschel.* Edited and introduced by Fritz Rothschild. New York: Free Press-Macmillan, 1965.

———. *The Circle of the Baal Shem Tov: Studies in Hasidism by A. J. Heschel.* Edited by Samuel Dresner. Chicago: University of Chicago Press, 1985.

———. *The Earth Is the Lord's: The Inner World of the Jew in Eastern Europe.* New York: Farrar, Straus and Giroux, 1978. Originally published, New York: Henry Schuman, 1950.

———. *God in Search of Man: A Philosophy of Judaism.* New York: Farrar, Straus and Giroux, 1955.

———. *I Asked for Wonder: A Spiritual Anthology.* Edited by Samuel Dresner. New York: Crossroads, 1983.

———. *The Insecurity of Freedom: Essays on Human Existence.* New York: Schocken, 1975.

———. *Israel: An Echo in Eternity.* Sixth printing. New York: Farrar, Straus and Giroux, 1974.

———. *Maimonides: A Biography.* Trans. Joachim Neugroschel. New York: Farrar, Straus and Giroux, 1982.

———. *Man Is Not Alone: A Philosophy of Religion.* New York: Farrar, Straus and Giroux, 1951.

———. *Man's Quest for God: Studies in Prayer and Symbolism.* New York: Scribner's, 1954.

———. *The Quest for Certainty in Saadia's Philosophy.* New York: Feldheim, 1944.

———. *A Passion for Truth.* New York: Farrar, Straus and Giroux, 1973.

———. *The Prophets.* New York: Harper & Row, 1962.

———. *The Sabbath: Its Meaning for Modern Man.* New York: Farrar, Straus and Young, 1951.

———. *Torah min ha-shamayim b'espakularia shel ha-dorot* (Theology of Ancient Judaism). 2 vols. London: Soncino, 1962–65.

———. *Who Is Man?* Stanford, California: Stanford University Press, 1965.

———. *The Wisdom of Heschel.* Edited by Ruth Marcus Goodhill. New York: Farrar, Straus and Giroux, 1975.

Heschel, Susannah, ed. *On Being a Jewish Feminist: A Reader.* New York: Schocken, 1983.

Hordern, William. *A Layman's Guide to Protestant Theology.* Revised Fourth Edition. New York: Macmillan, 1970.

Hunsinger, George, ed. and trans. *Karl Barth and Radical Politics.* Philadelphia: Westminster Press, 1976.

Husik, Issac. *A History of Medieval Jewish Philosophy.* New York: Atheneum, 1976.

Hutchinson, John A., et al., eds. *Christian Faith and Social Action.* New York: Scribners, 1953.

Janowsky, Oscar I., ed. *The American Jew: A Reappraisal, 1964.* Philadelphia: Jewish Publication Society, 1965.

Kallen, Horace. *Secularism Is the Will of God: An Essay in the Social Philosophy of Democracy and Religion.* New York: Twayne, 1954.

Kaplan, Mordecai. *Judaism as a Civilization: Toward a Reconstruction of American Jewish Life.* New York: Schocken, 1972.

———. *Judaism without Supernaturalism.* New York: Reconstructionist Press, 1958.

Kasimov, Harold. *Divine-Human Encounter: A Study of Abraham Joshua Heschel.* Washington, D.C.: University Press of America, 1979.

Katz, Steven. *Jewish Philosophers.* New York: Bloch, 1975.

Kaufman, William. *Contemporary Jewish Philosophers.* New York: Reconstructionist Press and Behrman, 1976.

Kegeley, Charles W. and Robert W. Bretall, eds. *Reinhold Niebuhr.* New York: Macmillan, 1956.

Klaperman, Gilbert. *The Story of Yeshiva University.* New York: Macmillan, 1969.

Kramer, Judith R., and Seymour Leventman. *Children of the Gilded Ghetto: Conflict Resolutions of Three Generations of American Jews.* New Haven: Yale University Press, 1961.

Kushner, Harold. *When Bad Things Happen to Good People.* New York: Schocken, 1981.

Lewisohn, Ludwig. *The Permanent Horizon.* New York and London: Harper & Brothers, 1934.

Mannheim, Karl. *Essays on the Sociology of Knowledge.* Edited and translated by Paul Kecskemeti. New York: Oxford University Press, 1952.

Mckelway, Alexander J. *The Systematic Theology of Paul Tillich: A Review and Analysis.* New York: Delta, 1964.

Merkle, John, ed. *Abraham Joshua Heschel: Exploring His Life and Thought.* New York: Macmillan, 1985.

———. *The Genesis of Faith: The Depth Theology of Abraham Joshua Heschel.* New York: Macmillan, 1985.

Merkley, Paul. *Reinhold Niebuhr: A Political Account.* Montreal: McGill Queen's University Press, 1975.

Mueller, David L. *Karl Barth.* Makers of the Modern Theological Mind Series, edited by Bob E. Patterson. Waco, Texas: Word Books, 1972.

Niebur, Reinhold. *Moral Man and Immoral Society: A Study in Ethics and Politics.* New York: Charles Scribner's Sons, 1932.

———. *The Nature and Destiny of Man: A Christian Interpretation.* 2 volumes. New York: Charles Scribner's Sons, I: 1941, II: 1943.

———. *Reflections of the End of an Era.* New York: Charles Scribner's Sons, 1934.

Novack, David and Norbert Samuelson, eds. *Creation and the End of Days: Judaism and Scientific Cosmology.* Proceedings of the 1984 Meeting of the Academy for Jewish Philosophy. New York: University Press of America, 1986.

Noveck, Simon. *Milton Steinberg: Portrait of a Rabbi.* New York: Ktav, 1978.

———, ed. *Great Jewish Thinkers of the Twentieth Century.* B'nai B'rith Great Books Series, 5 vols. Washington, D.C.: B'nai B'rith Department of Adult Jewish Education, 1963–67.

Nusan Porter, Jack, and Peter Dreier, eds. *Jewish Radicalism.* New York: Grove, 1973.

Patterson, Bob E. *Reinhold Niebuhr.* Texas: Word, Inc., 1977.

Petuchowski, Jacob. *Ever since Sinai: A Modern View of Torah.* New York: Scribe Publishing, 1961.

Plaut, Gunther. *The Growth of Reform Judaism: American and European Sources until 1948.* New York: World Union for Progressive Judaism, 1965.

Rackman, Emanuel. *One Man's Judaism.* Tel Aviv: Greenfield, 1978.

Ribalow, Harold U., ed. *Mid-Century.* New York: Beechurst Press, 1955.

Rose, P. I., ed. *The Ghetto and Beyond: Essays on Jewish Life in America.* New York: Random House, 1969.

Rosenack, Michael. "The Function of Contemporary Jewish Philosophy in the Con-
    struction of Religious Educational Theory in the Diaspora." (Hebrew). Ph.D.
    dissertation, Hebrew University of Jerusalem, 1976.
Rosenfield, Leonara Davidson (Cohen). *Portrait of a Philosopher*. New York: Har-
    court, Brace and World, 1962.
Rosenstock-Huessy, Eugen, ed. *Judaism Despite Christianity: The "Letters on Christianity
    and Judaism" between Eugen Rosenstock-Huessy and Franz Rosenzweig*. Translated
    by Dorothy Emmet. New York: Schocken, 1969.
Rosenzweig, Franz. *On Jewish Learning*. New York: Schocken, 1955.
———. *The Star of Redemption*. Translated by William W. Hallo. Boston: Beacon,
    1971.
Rothkoff, Aaron. *Bernard Revel: Builder of American Jewish Orthodoxy*. Philadelphia:
    Jewish Publication Society, 1972.
Rubenstein, Richard. *After Auschwitz: Radical Theology and Contemporary Judaism*. In-
    dianapolis: Bobbs-Merril, 1966.
———. *Power Struggle*. New York: Charles Scribner's Sons, 1974.
Samuelson, Norbert, ed. *Studies in Jewish Philosophy: Collected Essays of the Academy
    for Jewish Philosphy, 1980–1985*. New York: University Press of America, 1987.
Schilpp, Paul, and Maurice Friedman, eds. *The Philosophy of Martin Buber*. The Li-
    brary of Living Philosophers, vol. 12. La Salle, Illinois: Open Court, 1967.
Scholem, Gershom. *The Messianic Idea in Judaism and Other Essays in Jewish Spirituality*.
    Translated by Michael A. Meyer and Hillel Halkin. New York: Schocken,
    1971.
Scott, Nathan A., Jr., ed. *The Legacy of Reinhold Niebuhr*. Chicago: University of
    Chicago, 1974.
Sherwin, Byron. *Abraham Joshua Heschel*. Makers of Contemporary Theology Series.
    Atlanta: John Knox, 1979.
Sidorsky, David, ed. *The Future of the Jewish Community in America*. Philadelphia:
    Jewish Publication Society, 1973.
Siegel, Richard, Michael Strassfeld, and Sharon Strassfeld, eds. *The Jewish Catalog*.
    3 vols. Philadelphia: Jewish Publication Society, 1973–80.
Silver, Abba Hillel. *Where Judaism Differed*. New York: Collier-Macmillan, 1956.
Sklare, Marshall. *Conservative Judaism*. New York: Schocken, 1955.
———, ed. *The Jews: Patterns of an American Group*. New York: Free Press, 1958.
Sleeper, James, and Alan Mintz, eds. *The New Jews*. New York: Vintage, 1971.
Smart, James. *The Past, Present and Future of Biblical Theology*. Philadelphia: West-
    minster Press, 1979.
Soloveitchik, Joseph B. *Halakhic Man*. Translated by Lawrence Kaplan. Philadelphia:
    Jewish Publication Society, 1983.
———. *The Halakhic Mind: An Essay on Jewish Tradition and Modern Thought*. New
    York: Free Press, 1986.
———. *In Aloneness, in Togetherness: A Selection of Hebrew Writings of Rabbi Joseph B.
    Soloveitchik* (Hebrew). Edited by Pinchas Peli. Jerusalem: Orot, 1976.
———. *The Man of Halakha—Hidden and Revealed* (Hebrew). Jerusalem: World Zi-
    onist Organization, 1979.
———. *On Repentence in the Thought and Oral Discourses of Rabbi Joseph B. Soloveitchik*.
    Edited and reconstructed by Pinchas Peli. Jerusalem: Orot, Hebrew, 1975,
    English, 1980.
———. *The Rav Speaks: Five Addresses by Rabbi Joseph Soloveitchik*. Translated by S.
    M. Lehrman and A. H. Rabinowitz. Edited by David Telsner and Zvi Faier.
    Jerusalem: Orot, 1984.
———. *Reflections of the Rav: Lessons in Jewish Thought*. Edited by Abraham R. Besdin.
    Jerusalem: World Zionist Organization, 1979.

————. *Shiurei Harav: A Conspectus of the Public Lectures of Rabbi Joseph B. Soloveitchik.* Edited by Joseph Epstein. New York: Hamevaser, Yeshiva University, 1974.

Stampfer, Joshua, ed. *Prayer and Politics: The Twin Poles of Abraham Joshua Heschel.* Portland: Institute for Judaic Studies, 1985.

Steinberg, Milton. *Anatomy of Faith.* Edited by Arthur Cohen. New York: Harcourt, Brace & Company, 1960.

————. *As a Driven Leaf.* New York: Behrman, 1939.

————. *A Believing Jew,* Edited by Maurice Samuel. New York: Harcourt, Brace & Company, 1951.

Stone, Ronald. *Paul Tillich's Radical Social Thought.* Atlanta: John Knox Press, 1980.

Stumme, John. *Socialism in Theological Perspective: A Study of Paul Tillich, 1918–1933.* Ann Arbor: Scholars Press, 1978.

Tillich, Paul. *A History of Christian Thought: From Its Judaic and Hellenistic Origins to Existentialism.* Edited by Carl E. Braaten. New York: Simon and Schuster, 1967.

————. *The Interpretation of History.* Translated by N. A. Rasetzki and Elsa L. Talmey. New York: Charles Scribner's Sons, 1936.

————. *The Protestant Era.* Translated by James Luther Adams. Abridged edition. Chicago: University of Chicago Press, 1948.

————. *The Socialist Decision.* Translated by Franklin Sherman. New York: Harper and Row, 1977.

————. *Systematic Theology.* 3 vols. Chicago: University of Chicago Press, 1951–1963.

Weiman, Henry Nelson, ed. *Religious Liberals Reply.* Boston: Beacon, 1947.

Weiss-Rosmarin, Trude. *Religion of Reason: Hermann Cohen's System of Religious Philosophy.* New York: Bloch, 1936.

Wolf, Arnold, ed. *Rediscovering Judaism: Reflections on a New Theology.* Chicago: Quadrangle, 1965.

Wyschogrod, Michael. *The Body of Faith: Judaism as Corporeal Election.* Minneapolis: Seabury Press, 1983.

Zahrnt, Heinrich. *The Question of God: Protestant Theology in the 20th Century.* Translated by R. A. Wilson. New York: Harcourt, Brace & World, 1969.

Zeitlin, Joseph. *Disciples of the Wise: The Religious and Social Opinion of American Rabbis.* New York: Teacher's College of Columbia University, 1945.

B. ARTICLES

Agus, Jacob. "An Analysis of Milton Steinberg's '*Anatomy of Faith*'." *Conservative Judaism* 14 (Summer 1960): 1–4.

Altman, Alexander. "Franz Rosenzweig and Eugen Rosenstock- Huessy: An Introduction to Their 'Letters on Judaism and Christianity'." *Journal of Religion* 24 (October 1944): 258–270.

Ben Hamon (pseudonym). "The Reform Rabbis Debate Theology: A Report on the 1963 Meeting of the CCAR." *Judaism* 12 (Fall 1963): 479–486.

Ben-Horin, Meir. "The Ineffable: Critical Notes on Neo-Mysticism." *Jewish Quarterly Review* 46 (April 1956): 321–354.

————. "The Ultimate and the Mystery: A Critique of Some Neo-Mystical Tenets." *Jewish Quarterly Review* 51 (July 1960): 55–71; (October 1960): 141–156.

————. "Via Mystica." *Jewish Quarterly Review* 45 (January 1955): 249–258.

Berger, Bennett M. "How Long Is a Generation?" *British Journal of Sociology* 11 (March 1960): 10–23.

Berkovits, Eliezer. "Facing the Truth." *Judaism* 27 (Summer 1978): 324–326.

————. "Judaism in the Post-Christian Age." *Judaism* 15 (Winter 1966): 74–84.

Birnbaum, Ruth. "The Man of Dialogue and the Man of Halakhah." *Judaism* 26 (Winter 1977): 52–62.

Blau, Joseph L. "What's American About American Jewry?" *Judaism* 7 (Summer 1958): 208–218.

Borowitz, Eugene. "The Career of Jewish Existentialism." *Jewish Book Annual* 32 (1974–1975): 44–49.

————. "Crisis Theology and the Jewish Community." *Commentary* 32 (July 1961): 36–42.

————. "Existentialism's Meaning for Judaism." *Commentary* 28 (November 1959): 414–420.

————. "Faith and Method in Modern Jewish Theology." *Central Conference of American Rabbis Yearbook* 73 (1963): 215–228.

————. "The Jewish Need for Theology." *Commentary* 34 (August 1962): 138–144.

————. "On the *Commentary* Symposium: Alternatives in Creating a Jewish Apologetic." *Judaism* 15 (Fall 1966): 458–465.

————. "Reform Judaism's Fresh Awareness of Religious Problems: Theological Conference—Cincinnati 1950." *Commentary* 9 (June 1950): 567–572.

————. "The Typological Theology of Rabbi Joseph B. Soloveitchik." *Judaism* 15 (Spring 1966): 203–210.

Breslauer, Daniel. "Will Herberg: Intuitive Spokesman for American Judaism." *Judaism* 27 (Winter 1978): 7–12.

Cherbonnier, Edmond La B. "A. J. Heschel and the Philosophy of the Bible: Mystic or Rationalist?" *Commentary* 27 (January 1959): 23–29.

————. "Heschel as a Religious Thinker." *Conservative Judaism* 23 (Fall 1968): 25–39.

————. "Heschel's Time Bomb." *Conservative Judaism* 28 (Fall 1973): 10–18.

Cohen, Arthur. "An Analysis of Milton Steinberg's *Anatomy of Faith* Edited by Arthur Cohen: A Reply to the Critics." *Conservative Judaism* 14 (Summer 1960): 14–21.

————. "The Seminary and the Modern Rabbi." *Conservative Judaism* 13 (Spring 1959): 1–12.

Cohen, Elliot E. "Editorial Statement: An Act of Affirmation." *Commentary* 1 (November 1945): 1–3.

Cohon, Samuel S. "Existentialism and Judaism: Introductory Remarks." *Central Conference of American Rabbis Yearbook* 62 (1953): 399–401.

————. "The Existentialist Trend in Theology" in "Contemporary Currents in Jewish Theology: A Symposium." *Central Conference of American Rabbis Yearbook* 62 (1935): 343–385.

————. "The Future Task of Jewish Theology." *Reconstructionist* 28 (January 10, 1958): 20–24.

Dewey, John. "Anti-Naturalism in Extremis." *Partisan Review* 10 (January-February 1943): 24–40.

Eisen, Arnold. "Theology, Sociology, Ideology: Jewish Thought in America, 1925–1955." *Modern Judaism* 2 (February 1982): 91–103.

Eisenstein, Ira. "An Analysis of Milton Steinberg's 'Anatomy of Faith'." *Conservative Judaism* 14 (Summer 1960): 5–14.

Fackenheim, Emil. "Can We Believe in Judaism Religiously?" *Commentary* 6 (December 1948): 521–527.

————. "Hermann Cohen: After Fifty Years," *Leo Baeck Memorial Lecture* 12 (New York: Leo Baeck Institute, 1969): 1–27.

————. "Judaism, Christianity, and Reinhold Niebuhr: A Reply to Levi Olan." *Judaism* 5 (Fall 1956): 316–324.

———. "Kant and Radical Evil." *University of Toronto Quarterly* 23 (July 1954): 339–353.

———. "Liberalism and Reform Judaism." *Central Conference of American Rabbis Journal* no. 21 (April 1958): 1–17.

———. "Martin Buber's Concept of Revelation." In *The Philosophy of Martin Buber*, ed. Maurice Friedman and Arthur Schilpp. LaSalle, Illinois: Open Court, 1967. 273–296.

———. "The Modern Jew's Path to God: Initiating the Great Encounter." *Commentary* 9 (May 1950): 450–457.

———. "The Possibility of the Universe in Al-Farabi, Ibn Sina, and Maimonides." *Proceedings of the American Academy of Jewish Research* 16 (1947): 39–70.

———. Review of *God in Search of Man*, by Abraham Joshua Heschel. *Conservative Judaism* 15 (Fall 1960): 50–53.

———. Review of *Judaism and Modern Man*, by Will Herberg. *Judaism* 1 (April 1952): 172–176.

———. Review of *Judaism: A Way of Life*, by Samuel S. Cohon. *Commentary* 3 (September 1949): 302–304.

———. Review of *Man Is Not Alone*, by Abraham Joshua Heschel. *Judaism* 1 (January 1952): 85–89.

———. "Schelling's Conception of Positive Philosophy." *Review of Metaphysics* 7 (June 1954): 563–582.

———. "Some Recent Rationalistic Reactions to the 'New Jewish Theology'." *Central Conference of American Rabbis Journal* no. 26 (June 1959): 42–48.

———. "The State of Jewish Belief: A Symposium." *Commentary* 42 (August 1966): 87–89.

Fischoff, Ephraim. "Judaism and Modern Theology." *Central Conference of American Rabbis Yearbook* 66 (1956): 216–230.

Fox, Marvin. "Heschel, Intuition, and the Halakhah." *Tradition* 3 (Fall 1960): 5–15.

———. "Kierkegaard and Rabbinic Judaism." *Judaism* 2 (April 1953): 160–169.

Friedman, Maurice. "Abraham Joshua Heschel: Toward a Philosophy of Judaism." *Conservative Judaism* 10 (Winter 1956): 1–10.

Frimer, Norman. "The A-Theological Judaism of the American Jewish Community." *Judaism* 11 (Spring 1962): 144–154.

Gittelson, Natalie. "American Jews Rediscover Orthodoxy." *New York Times Magazine* 30 September 1984.

Glatzer, Nahum. "Franz Rosenzweig." *Yivo Annual of Jewish Social Science* 1 (1946): 107–133.

———. Review of *Judaism and Modern Man*, by Will Herberg. *Commentary* 13 (March 19): 296–298.

Glicksberg, Charles I. "Religious Attitudes of Jewish Youth." *Congress Weekly* 23 (February 6, 1956): 10–12.

Goldberg, Hillel. "Abraham Joshua Heschel and His Times." *Midstream* 28 (April 1982): 36–42.

———. "Soloveitchik's Lonely Quest." *Midstream* 28 (November 1982): 31–32.

Gordis, Robert. "The Genesis of *Judaism*: A Chapter in Jewish Cultural History." *Judaism* 30 (Fall 1981): 390–395.

———. Review of *Anatomy of Faith*, by Milton Steinberg. *New York Times Sunday Book Review* 10 April 1960.

———. "The Tasks before Us: A Preface to Our Journal." *Conservative Judaism* 1 (January 1945): 1–8.

———. "Toward a Renascence of Judaism." *Judaism* 1 (January 1952): 3–10.

Gumbiner, Joseph. 'Existentialism and Father Abraham: A Colloquy with Kierkegaard." *Commentary* 5 (February 1948): 143–148.

Halevi, Jacob. "Kierkegaard and the Midrash." *Judaism* 4 (Winter 1955): 13–28.

Halpern, Ben. "Apologia contra Rabbines." *Midstream* 11 (Spring 1956): 23–30.

Hartman, David. "The Breakdown of Tradition and the Quest for Renewal: Re-flections on Three Jewish Responses to Modernity. Part 4: Abraham Joshua Heschel." *Forum* 39 (Fall 1980): 61–75.

———. "The Breakdown of Tradition and the Quest for Renewal: Reflections on Three Jewish Responses to Modernity. Part 1: J. B. Soloveitchik." *Forum* 37 (Spring 1980): 10–23.

Heller, Bernard. "Report of the Commission on Jewish Theology." *Central Conference of American Rabbis Yearbook* 66 (1956): 68–70.

Herberg, Will. "Americans' New Religiousness: A Way of Belonging or the Way of God?" *Commentary* 20 (September 1955): 240–247.

———. "Athens and Jerusalem: Confrontations and Dialogue." *Drew Gateway* 28 (Spring 1958): 178–196.

———. "From Marxism to Judaism." *Commentary* 3 (January 1947): 25–32.

———. "Has Judaism Still Power to Speak? A Religion for an Age of Crisis." *Commentary* 7 (May 1949): 447–457.

———. "Historicism as Touchstone." *Christian Century* 77 (March 16, 1960): 311–313.

———. "Judaism as Personal Decision." *Conservative Judaism* 22 (Summer 1968): 9–20.

———. "The Postwar Revival of the Synagogue: Does It Reflect a Religious Reawakening?" *Commentary* 9 (April 1950): 315–325.

———. "Prophetic Faith in an Age of Crisis." *Judaism* 1 (July 1952): pp. 195–202.

———. "Reinhold Niebuhr: Christian Apologist to the Secular World." *Union Seminary Quarterly* 11 (October 1956): 11–16.

———. "The Religious Stirrings on the Campus." *Commentary* 13 (March 1952): 242–244.

———. "Religious Trends in American Jewry." *Judaism* 3 (Summer 1954): 229–240.

———. Review of *A Believing Jew: The Selected Writings of Milton Steinberg.* Ed. Maurice Samuel. *Commentary* 12 (November 1951): 498.

———. Review of *God in Search of Man* by A. J. Heschel. *Christian Century* 73 (April 18, 1956): 486.

———. "Rosenzweig's 'Judaism of Personal Existence': A Third Way Between Orthodoxy and Modernism." *Commentary* 6 (December 1950): 541–549.

———. "The Strangeness of Faith." In *Faith Enacted as History: Essays in Biblical Theology by Will Herberg.* Ed. and intro., Bernhard Anderson. Philadelphia: Westminster Press, 1976. 9–28.

———. "Theological Problems of the Hour." *Proceedings of the Rabbinical Assembly of America* 13 (1949): 409–428.

———. "What Is Jewish Religion? Reflections on Rabbi Philip Bernstein's Article in *Life.*" *Jewish Frontier* 17 (October 1950): 8–13.

Heschel, Abraham J. "No Religion Is an Island." *Union Seminary Quarterly Review* 21 (January 1966): 117–134.

———. "On Prayer." *Conservative Judaism* 25 (Fall 1970): 3–12.

———. "Reinhold Niebuhr: A Last Farewell." *Conservative Judaism* 25 (Summer 1971): 62–63.

———. "The Spirit of Prayer." *Proceedings of the Rabbinical Assembly of America* 17 (1953): 151–178.

———. "Teaching Jewish Theology in the Solomon Schechter Day School." *The Synagogue School* 28 (Fall 1969): 4–33.

————. "Toward an Understanding of Halacha." *The Central Conference of American Rabbis Yearbook* 63 (1953): 386–409.

————. "What We Might Do Together." *Religious Education* 52 (March-April 1967): 133–140.

Himmelfarb, Milton. Introduction to "The State of Jewish Belief: A Symposium." *Commentary* 42 (August 1966): 71–72.

Hook, Sidney. "The New Failure of Nerve." *The Partisan Review* 10 (January-February 1943): 2–23.

Hyman, Paula. "An Interview with Paula Hyman." *The Jewish Week* (September 17, 1982).

Hyslop, Ralph Douglas. "How Relevant Is Reinhold Neibuhr?" *Judaism* 15 (Fall 1966): 419–425.

Kaplan, Edward. "Language and Reality in Abraham J. Heschel's Philosophy of Religion." *Journal of the American Academy of Religion* 41 (March 1973): 94–113.

————. "Mysticism and Despair in Abraham J. Heschel's Religious Thought." *Journal of Religion* 57 (January 1977): 33–47.

————. "The Religious Philosophy of Rabbi Joseph Soloveitchik." *Tradition* 14 (Fall 1983): 43–63.

Kaplan, Mordecai. "If Theology Were Our Only Métier." *Conservative Judaism* 11 (Winter 1957): 20–25.

Karff, Samuel. "The Agada as a Source of Contemporary Jewish Theology." *Central Conference of American Rabbis Yearbook* 73 (1963): 191–198.

Karp, Abraham. "Toward a Theology for Conservative Judaism." *Conservative Judaism* 10 (Summer 1956): 14–21.

Katz, Steven. "A. J. Heschel and Hasidism." *The Journal of Jewish Studies* 31 (Spring 1980): 82–104.

————. "Jewish Philosophy in the 1980s: A Diagnosis and Prescription." *Studies in Jewish Philosophy* 1. Melrose Park, Pennsylvania: Academy for Jewish Philosophy (1980): 33–54.

Kaufmann, Walter. "The Reception of Existentialism in the United States." Special Issue: "The Legacy of the German Refugee Intellectuals." *Salmagundi* 3 (Fall/Winter 1969–70): 69–96.

Kohn, Eugene. "Existentialism Re-examined." *Reconstructionist* 32 (October 14, 1966): 7–9.

————. "The Menace of Existentialist Religion." *Reconstructionist* 17 (January 11, 1952): 7–15.

————. "Prayer for the Modern Jew." *Proceedings of the Rabbinical Assembly of America* 17 (1953): 179–191.

Kohn, Jakob. "The Assault on Reason." *Reconstructionst* 23 (January 24, 1958): 7–12.

Konvitz, Milton. Review of *Judaism and Modern Man,* by Will Herberg. *Saturday Review of Literature* (March 8, 1952): 57–58.

Kristol, Irving. "How Basic Is 'Basic Judaism'?" *Commentary* 5 (January 1948): 27–34.

Kurzweil, Z'vi. "Universalism in the Philosophy of Rabbi Joseph B. Soloveitchik." *Judaism* 31 (Fall 1982): 459–471.

Kushner, Harold. "The American-Jewish Experience: A Conservative Perspective." *Judaism* 31 (Summer 1982): 296–298.

Lasker, Arnold. "Personal Prayer." *Proceedings of the Rabbinical Assembly of America* 17 (1953): 231–238.

Leibman, Charles. "Left and Right in American Orthodoxy." *Judaism* 15 (Winter 1966): 102–107.

———. "The Orthodox Left: A Reply." *Conservative Judaism* 20 (Winter 1966): 47–52.

———. "Orthodoxy in American Jewish Life." *American Jewish Yearbook* 66 (1965): 21–92.

———. "The Training of American Rabbis." *American Jewish Yearbook* 69 (1968): 3–112.

Lewisohn, Ludwig. Review of *Judaism and Modern Man*, by Will Herberg. *Congress Weekly* 18 (October 8, 1951): 13–14.

Lookstein, Joseph. "The Neo-Hasidism of Abraham J. Heschel." *Judaism* 5 (Summer 1956): 248–255.

Lowith, Karl. "M. Heidegger and F. Rosenzweig." *Philosophy and Phenomenological Research* 3 (September 1942): 53–77.

Martin, Bernard. "Conservative Judaism and Reconstructionism in the Last Three Decades." *Journal of Reform Judaism* 25 (Spring 1978): 95–152.

Meyer, Michael. "Judaism after Auschwitz: The Religious Thought of Emil L. Fackenheim." *Commentary* 53 (June 1972): 55–62.

Narot, Joseph. "Recent Jewish Existentialist Writing." *Central Conference of American Rabbis Yearbook* 62 (1953): 435–444.

———. "Two Authoritarian Critics of Psychoanalysis." *Reconstructionist* 18 (May 16, 1952): 7–13.

Neusner, Jacob. "The New Orthodox Left." *Conservative Judaism* 20 (Fall 1965): 10–18.

Niebuhr, Reinhold. Review of *Man Is Not Alone*, by A. J. Heschel. *New York Herald Tribune Book Reviews* (April 1, 1951).

Novak, David. "In Memoriam: Professor Samuel Atlas (1899–1977)." *Journal of Reform Judaism* 28 (Winter 1981): 92–94.

Noveck, Simon. "Milton Steinberg's Philosophy of Religion." *Judaism* 26 (Winter 1977): 35–45.

Olan, Levi. "Reinhold Niebuhr and the Hebraic Spirit: A Critical Inquiry." *Judaism* 5 (Spring 1956): 108–122.

Oppenheim, Michael. "Eliezer Schweid: A Philosophy of Return." *Judaism* 35 (Winter 1986): 66–77.

Peli, Pinchas. "Heschel and the Hassidic Tradition." In *Prayer and Politics: The Twin Poles of Abraham Joshua Heschel*, edited by Joshua Stampfer. Portland: Institute for Judaic Studies, 1985. 63–84.

———. "Repentant Man: A High Level in Rabbi Soloveitchik's Typology of Man." *Tradition* 18 (Summer 1980): 135–159.

———. "Soloveitchik from an Israeli Perspective." *Midstream* 28 (November 1982): 35–38.

Petuchowski, Jakob. "Faith as the Leap of Action: The Theology of Abraham Joshua Heschel." *Commentary* 25 (May 1958): 390–397.

———. "The Question of Jewish Theology." *Judaism* 7 (Winter 1958): 49–55.

Plotkin, Albert. "Abraham Joshua Heschel: A Tribute." *Central Conference of American Rabbis Journal* 20 (Summer 1973): 75–79.

Podhoretz, Norman. "The Intellectuals and Jewish Fate." *Midstream* 3 (Winter 1957): 15–23.

———. Introduction to "Jewishness and the Younger Intellectuals: A Symposium." *Commentary* 31 (April 1961): 306–310.

———. "Jewish Culture and the Intellectuals." *Commentary* 19 (May 1955): 451–457.

———, ed. "Under Forty: A Symposium on American Literature and the Younger Generation of American Jews." *Contemporary Jewish Record* (February 1944): 3–37.

Rackman, Emanuel. "Orthodox Judaism Moves with the Times." *Commentary* 13 (June 1952): 545–550.

———. "Soloveitchik: On Differing with My Rebbe." *Sh'ma* (March 8, 1985): 65.

Rosenberg, Harold. "Pledged to the Marvelous: An Open Letter to Will Herberg." *Commentary* 3 (February 1947): 145–151.

Rotenstreich, Nathan. "On Prophetic Consciousness." *The Journal of Religion* 54 (July 1974): 185–198.

Rothschild, Fritz. "Architect and Herald of a New Theology." *Conservative Judaism* 28 (Fall 1973): 55–60.

———. "Conservative Judaism Faces the Need for Change: In What Direction, How Much, and How?" *Commentary* 16 (November 1953): 447–455.

———. "Herberg as Jewish Theologian." *National Review* 29 (August 1977): 885–886.

Samuelson, Norbert. "Introduction: The Academy for Jewish Philosophy." *Studies in Jewish Philosophy* 1. Melrose Park, Pennsylvania: Academy for Jewish Philosophy (1980): 5–9.

Schneider, Herbert W. "On Reading Heschel's *God in Search of Man:* A Review Article." *The Review of Religion* 21 (November 1956): 31–38.

Schumer, Fran. "A Return to Religion." *New York Times Magazine* 15, April 1984.

Schwarzschild, Steven. "Judaism à la Mode." *The Menorah Journal* 40 (Spring 1952): 102–121.

———. "The Role and Limits of Reason in Contemporary Jewish Theology." *Central Conference of American Rabbis Yearbook* 73 (1963): 199–214.

Sherman, H. "Three Generations." *Jewish Frontier* 21 (July 1954): 12–16.

Siegel, Seymour. "Mordecai Kaplan in Retrospect." *Commentary* 74 (July 1982): 58–61.

———. "Theology, Torah, and the Man of Today." *Conservative Judaism* 16 (Winter/Spring 1962): 56–66.

———. "A Tribute to Will Herberg: A Biographical Sketch." *National Review* 29 (August 5, 1977): 880–881.

———. "Will Herberg (1902–1977): A Baal Teshuvah Who Became a Theologian, Sociologist, Teacher." *American Jewish Yearbook* 78 (1978): 529–537.

Silberman, Lou. "Concerning Jewish Theology in North America: Some Notes on a Decade." *American Jewish Yearbook* 70 (1969): 37–58.

———. "The Philosophy of Abraham Joshua Heschel." *Jewish Heritage* 2 (Spring 1959): 23–26.

———. "The Theologian's Task." *Central Conference of American Rabbis Yearbook* 73 (1963): 173–190.

Silverman, David Wolf. "Current Theological Trends: A Survey and an Analysis." *Proceedings of the Rabbinical Assembly of America* 23 (1959): 71–100.

Singer, David and Moshe Sokol. "Joseph Soloveitchik: Lonely Man of Faith." *Modern Judaism* 2 (October 1982): 227–272.

Soloveitchik, Joseph. "Confrontation." *Tradition* 6 (Spring/Summer 1964): 5–30.

———. "Ish Ha-Halakhah." *Talpiot* 1:3–4 (1944): 651–735.

———. "The Lonely Man of Faith." *Tradition* 7 (Summer 1965): 5–67.

———. "The Sacred and Profane: Kodesh and Chol in World Perspective." *Hazedek* (May-June, 1945): 4–20.

Sosevsky, Morris. "The Lonely Man of Faith Confronts the Ish Ha-Halakhah: An Analysis of the Critique of Rabbi Joseph B. Soloveitchik's Philosophical Writings." *Tradition* 16 (Fall 1976): 73–89.

Spero, Shubert. Review of "The Condition of Jewish Belief: A Symposium." *Tradition* 9 (Fall 1967): 141–147.

————. Review of *Ever since Sinai,* by Jakob Petuchowski. *Tradition* 5 (Fall 1962): 102–106.

————. "Stirrings in Reform Theology." *The Jewish Observer* 1 (May 1964): 13–15.

Spitzer, Alan B. "The Historical Problem of Generations." *American Historical Review* 78 (December 1973): 1353–1385.

Steinberg, Milton. "Kierkegaard and Judaism." *Menorah Journal* 37 (Spring 1949): 163–180.

————. "The Outlook of Reinhold Niebuhr: A Description and Appraisal." *Reconstructionist* 11 (December 14, 1945): 10–15.

————. Review of "From Marxism to Judaism," by Will Herberg. *Park Avenue Synagogue Bulletin* 1 (February 17, 1947): 2.

————. "The Theological Issues of the Hour." *Proceedings of the Rabbinical Assembly of America* 13 (1949): 356–408.

Stone, Ronald. "The Zionism of Paul Tillich and Reinhold Neibuhr." *Jewish Digest* (March-April 1983): 8–16.

Teller, Judd. "A Critique of the New Jewish Theology: From a Secularist Point of View." *Commentary* 25 (March 1958): 243–252.

Tillich, Paul. "Beyond Religious Socialism: How My Mind Has Changed in the Last Decade." *Christian Century* 66 (June 15, 1949): 732–733.

Weisberg, Harold. "Escape from Reason: A Reply to Will Herberg." *Reconstructionist* 16 (December 1, 1950): 17–24.

Weiss-Rosmarin, Trude. "Jewish Theology." *Jewish Spetator* 25 (November 1960): 5–7.

Werblowsky, R. J. Zwi. "A Note on the Relations between Judaism and Christianity." *Forum for the Problems of Zionism, Jewry, and the State of Israel: Proceedings of the Jerusalem Ideological Conference* 4 (1959): 54–59.

Wolfe, Arnold. "On My Mind." *Sh'ma* (September 19, 1975): 295.

Wurtzberger, Walter. "The State of Orthodoxy: A Symposium." *Tradition* 20 (Spring 1982): 3–5.

Zuckerman, Arthur. "More on *Anatomy of Faith.*" *Reconstructionist* 26 (January 27, 1961): 24–26.

C. *CONVERSATIONS*

Berkovits, Eliezer. May 1978.
Finkelstein, Louis. 19 January 1982.
Greenberg, Simon. 14 August 1982.
Hyman, Arthur. 6 November 1980.
Kaplan, Mordecai. 5 July 1964.
Lieberman, Saul. 9 June 1981.
Matt, Hershel. 4 May 1981.
————. 13 December 1982.
Muffs, Yochanan. 14 May 1982.
Registrar, Yeshiva University. 9 July 1982.
Rothschild, Fritz. 5 October 1982.
Siegel, Seymour. 5 October 1982.
————. 1 December 1982.

D. *LETTERS*

1. Letters in the Will Herberg Archives, Drew University, Madison, New Jersey.
Herberg, Will. Letter to Hershel Matt. 18 August 1947.
————. 7 December 1947.
————. 2 December 1948.
————. 17 October 1949.
————. 2 November 1949.
————. 7 July 1950.
————. 18 December 1950
————. 8 March 1951.
————. 9 May 1951.
————. 25 October 1951.
————. 19 March 1952.
————. 7 April 1952.
————. 6 August 1952.
————. 12 November 1955.
————. 28 February 1956.
2. Letters in Journals
Cohen, Arthur. Letter. "Correspondence: On Steinberg's *Anatomy of Faith.*" *Reconstructionist* 27 (February 24, 1961): 27–28.
Fackenheim, Emil. Letter. "Correspondence: For and Against Herberg." *Jewish Frontier* 17 (November 1950): 29.
Gittelsohn, Roland. Letter. "The 'New Theology'." *Commentary* 25 (May 1958): 445.
Goldstein, Albert. Letter. "Correspondence: For and Against Herberg." *Jewish Frontier* 17 (November 1950): 29.
Gordis, Robert. Letter. *Commentary* 3 (May 1947): 490–491.
Konwitz, Milton. Letter. "Correspondence: For and Against Herberg." *Jewish Frontier* 17 (November 1950): 29.
Petuchowski, Jakob. Letter. "Jewish Theology." *Jewish Spectator* 26 (January 1961): 23–24.
Sandmel, Samuel. Letter. "Correspondence: For and Against Herberg." *Jewish Frontier* 17 (November 1950): 28.
Siegel, Seymour. Letter. "The 'New Theology.'" *Commentary* 25 (May 1958): 444.

INDEX